Eating the
Honey of Words

Also by Robert Bly

Poetry:

Morning Poems
Meditations on the Insatiable Soul
The Man in the Black Coat Turns
What Have I Ever Lost by Dying?
Loving a Woman in Two Worlds
The Light Around the Body
Silence in the Snowy Fields

Anthologies:

The Rag and Bone Shop of the Heart
News of the Universe
The Soul Is Here for Its Own Joy

Prose:

American Poetry: Wildness and Domesticity
Iron John
The Sibling Society
The Maiden King (with Marion Woodman)

EATING THE HONEY OF WORDS

New and Selected Poems

—⁓—

Robert Bly

HarperFlamingo
An Imprint of HarperCollins*Publishers*

The poems in this volume previously appeared in the following collections: *Silence in the Snowy Fields,* Wesleyan University Press, 1962; *The Light Around the Body,* Harper & Row, 1967; *The Morning Glory,* Kayak Editions, 1969; *The Teeth Mother Naked at Last,* City Lights, 1970; *Sleepers Joining Hands,* Harper & Row, 1973; *The Point Reyes Poems,* Mudra, 1974; *The Morning Glory* (enlarged edition), Harper & Row, 1975; *This Body Is Made of Camphor and Gopherwood,* Harper & Row, 1977; *This Tree Will Be Here for a Thousand Years,* Harper & Row, 1977, revised 1992; *The Man in the Black Coat Turns,* Dial Press, 1981; *Loving a Woman in Two Worlds,* Dial Press, 1985; *Selected Poems,* Harper & Row, 1986; *Angels of Pompeii,* Ballantine, 1991; *What Have I Ever Lost By Dying?,* HarperCollins, 1992; *Meditations on the Insatiable Soul,* HarperCollins, 1994; *Morning Poems,* HarperCollins, 1997.

My grateful acknowledgment to the editors of the following publications in which the new poems in this volume were published:

"Poem for Eudalia," *Lapis;* "Going Home with the World," *The Nation;* "Driving West in 1970," *Poetry;* "A Pint of Whiskey and Five Cigars," *The Progressive;* "A Poem Beginning with a Line by Seal Scholars" and "Love Poem About a Spinning Wheel," *Blue Sofa Review;* "Blessings on the Body's Inner Furnace," *Michigan Review.*

HarperCollins books may be purchased for educational, business, or sales promotional use. For information please write: Special Markets Department, HarperCollins Publishers, Inc., 10 East 53rd Street, New York, NY 10022.

FIRST EDITION

Designed by William Ruoto

Library of Congress Cataloging-in-Publication Data

Bly, Robert
    Eating the honey of words : new and selected poems / Robert Bly—
  1st ed.
     p. cm.
    ISBN 0-06-017562-1
  PS3552.L9E28 1999
  811'.54—dc21   98-51152

99 00 01 02 03 ❖ /HC 10 9 8 7 6 5 4 3 2 1

EATING THE HONEY OF WORDS

New and Selected Poems

—◆—

Robert Bly

HarperFlamingo
An Imprint of HarperCollinsPublishers

The poems in this volume previously appeared in the following collections: *Silence in the Snowy Fields,* Wesleyan University Press, 1962; *The Light Around the Body,* Harper & Row, 1967; *The Morning Glory,* Kayak Editions, 1969; *The Teeth Mother Naked at Last,* City Lights, 1970; *Sleepers Joining Hands,* Harper & Row, 1973; *The Point Reyes Poems,* Mudra, 1974; *The Morning Glory* (enlarged edition), Harper & Row, 1975; *This Body Is Made of Camphor and Gopherwood,* Harper & Row, 1977; *This Tree Will Be Here for a Thousand Years,* Harper & Row, 1977, revised 1992; *The Man in the Black Coat Turns,* Dial Press, 1981; *Loving a Woman in Two Worlds,* Dial Press, 1985; *Selected Poems,* Harper & Row, 1986; *Angels of Pompeii,* Ballantine, 1991; *What Have I Ever Lost By Dying?,* HarperCollins, 1992; *Meditations on the Insatiable Soul,* HarperCollins, 1994; *Morning Poems,* HarperCollins, 1997.

My grateful acknowledgment to the editors of the following publications in which the new poems in this volume were published:

"Poem for Eudalia," *Lapis;* "Going Home with the World," *The Nation;* "Driving West in 1970," *Poetry;* "A Pint of Whiskey and Five Cigars," *The Progressive;* "A Poem Beginning with a Line by Seal Scholars" and "Love Poem About a Spinning Wheel," *Blue Sofa Review;* "Blessings on the Body's Inner Furnace," *Michigan Review.*

HarperCollins books may be purchased for educational, business, or sales promotional use. For information please write: Special Markets Department, HarperCollins Publishers, Inc., 10 East 53rd Street, New York, NY 10022.

FIRST EDITION

Designed by William Ruoto

Library of Congress Cataloging-in-Publication Data

Bly, Robert
    Eating the honey of words : new and selected poems / Robert Bly—
    1st ed.
      p. cm.
     ISBN 0-06-017562-1
    PS3552.L9E28 1999
    811'.54—dc21   98-51152

99 00 01 02 03 ❖ /HC 10 9 8 7 6 5 4 3 2 1

For Mary, Wesley, Bridget, Noah, Micah,
and Sam

CONTENTS

III: The Light Around the Body (1957–70)

VII: This Body Is Made of Camphor and Gopherwood (1973–80)

VIII: The Man in the Black Coat Turns (1980–84)

IX: Meditations on the Insatiable Soul (1990–94)

X: Morning Poems (1993–97)

XI: New Poems (1997–98)

I
EARLY POEMS
1950–55

SEASONS IN THE NORTH WOODS

1

The wheeling blue-bill mallards all night long
With whistling wings curve down from gravelly clouds,
While down below them, crazed on the chill lakes,
The loons shake out their wings, dive down, and rise,
Cry back up in reply. The Star that reaches
Far past the Chair and the rush of Charles's Wain,
Bends down, and pondering in the blaze of night,
Lifts fish from chill pits into April streams.

2

Cracking weed shells, and thwacking bills on bark,
The agile companies of April sit
As quaint and graceful as medieval guilds.
Now the ruffed grouse beat their wings on rotting logs,
And throb the spring away. Farmers dig holes,
And women bring their lunch through wooded paths.
Standing among the popple, the old hired man
Hoists stones, and lifts his shirttail to his face.

3

Then soon, how soon, the summer's days are gone;
And blackbirds form in flocks, their duties through.
And now the last autumnal freedom comes:
Zumbrota acorns drop, sun-pushed as plums,
To half-wild hogs in Cerro Gordo trees,

And disappointed bees, with half-gold knees
Sail home. It's done. October's cold is sweet,
And winter will be stamping of the feet.

A HOME IN DARK GRASS

In the deep fall the body awakes
And we find lions on the seashore—
Nothing to fear.
The wind rises; the water is born,
Spreading white tomb-clothes on a rocky shore,
Drawing us up
From the bed of the land.

We did not come to remain whole.
We came to lose our leaves like the trees,
Trees that start again,
Drawing up from the great roots.
So men captured by the Moors
Wake, rowing in the cold ocean
Air, living a second life.

That we should learn of poverty and rags,
That we should taste the weed of Dillinger,
And swim in the sea,
Not always walking on dry land,
And, dancing, find in the trees a savior,
A home in dark grass,
And nourishment in death.

LIVING IN THE FIRE

No teak, nor piracies of marble
Can match this pain,
Not diamonds nor thyme
Nor smoke of hyacinth
No emeralds reach this pain,
Which is gorgeous
Oh Abraham! More than choirs
Of teak or the owls of Spain.

WHEN THE DUMB SPEAK

There's a joyful night in which we lose
Everything, and drift
Like a radish
Rising and falling, and the ocean at last
Throws us into the ocean;
In that ocean we are sinking
As if floating on darkness.
The body raging,
And driving itself, disappearing in smoke:
Walks in large cities late at night,
Reading the Bible in Christian Science windows,
Or reading a history of Bougainville:
Then the images appear—
Images of grief,
Images of the body shaken in the grave,
And the graves filled with seawater;
Fires in the sea,
Bodies smoldering like ships,
Images of wasted life,
Life lost, imagination ruined,
The house fallen,
The gold sticks broken!
Then shall the talkative be silent
And the dumb will speak.

WHERE WE MUST LOOK FOR HELP

The dove returns; it found no resting place;
It was in flight all night above the shaken seas.
Beneath Ark eaves
The dove shall magnify the tiger's bed;
Give the dove peace.
The split-tail swallows leave the sill at dawn;
At dusk blue swallows shall return.
On the third day the crow shall fly;
The crow, the crow, the spider-colored crow,
The crow shall find new mud to walk upon.

A Dispute

The Lazy Man: In my dream I saw flowers.
    White flowers covered the hill.
    When I came near, I saw
    Swords lay among the flowers.

The Tense Man: And I have cut the stony spur
    That laid unruly arms on the lawn,
    And cut to make that sure
    Green energy be gone.

The Lazy Man: When the sweet man dies, stabbed
    By the boar, and his blood
    Darkens the river, young girls
    Beat their small breasts and cry.

The Tense Man: If love, girl love, is but a jaunt,
    A fall that journeys to no spring,
    Then who will make the loaves
    And cry the calls to prayer?

The Lazy Man: I saw flowers in my dream.
    White flowers covered the hill.
    When I came near, I saw
    Swords lay among the flowers.

AWAKENING

We are approaching sleep: the chestnut blossoms in
    the mind
Mingle with thoughts of pain,
And the long roots of barley, bitterness
As of the oak roots staining the water dark
In Louisiana, the wet streets soaked with rain
And sodden blossoms, out of this
We have come, a tunnel softly hurtling into darkness.

The storm is coming. The small farmhouse in
    Minnesota
Is hardly strong enough for the storm.
Darkness, darkness in the grasses, darkness in trees.
Even the water in wells trembles.
Bodies give off darkness, and chrysanthemums
Are dark, and horses, who are bearing great loads of hay
To the deep barns where the dark air is moving from
    the corners.

Lincoln's statue, and the traffic. From the long past
Into the long present
A bird forgotten in these pressures, warbling,
As the great wheel turns around, grinding
The living in water.
Washing, continual washing, in water now stained
With blossoms and rotting logs, cries half-
Muffled, from beneath the earth, the living finally as
    awake as the dead.

UNREST

A strange unrest hovers over the nation:
This is the last dance, the wild tossing of Morgan's
    seas,
The division of spoils.
A lassitude enters into the diamonds
Of the body. In high school the explosion begins,
The child is partly killed. When the fight is over,
And the land and the sea
Ruined, two shapes inside us rise, and move away.

But the baboon whistles on the shores of death—
Climbing and falling, tossing nuts and stones,
He gambols by the tree
Whose branches hold the expanses of cold,
The planets whirling and the black sun,
The cries of insects, and the tiny slaves
In the prisons of bark:
Charlemagne, we are approaching your islands!

We are returning now to the snowy trees,
Charlemagne, through which you rode all night
With stiff hands. Now
The darkness is falling, in which we sleep
And wake, a darkness in which thieves shudder
And the insane have a hunger for snow,
And stiff-faced men like me
Fall on their knees in the dungeons of sleep.

THREE CHORAL STANZAS

1

I have gone down the old Tobacco Trail;
All over Tennessee the dead stand up
And shake the briars out of ballad bones!
Those torn in Shiloh meadows come alive.
I saw the worms march into Cumberland
And slumbering trees shout out the welcome there
To shrouds approaching from the Donner Pass.

2

The moon shines down on the Spanish battlefield.
There crumpled, trampled, pierced, or prone and
    whole,
The pale steel knights lie dead in weeds and gleam,
Friends raise them up, remove the bowels and lungs,
And in the cavities lay evergreens.
Tenderly they lift the dead to wagon-floors,
And men with wounds are bound on boughs of pine.

3

We write long poems, and make high towers, because
Those traveling to the grave do not return.
What has wild Pliny sent back since he died?
And dust has muffled Blackhawk's awkward tongue.
The dead do not come back; it is because
No word returns that we will never give in,
Nor without crowns will we be satisfied.

A Poem for the Drunkard President

Columbus guessed that below the Jamaican hills
There were cobalt porcelains, Geese Flying
Amid Three Clouds, Shang incense burners,
Hares made of gold pounding jade rice.
He died in chains, in a dungeon, growling like a dog.
Coronado, hankering for Cibola's cities, inquired
Of the Cherokees. They said, "Go to Kansas." His men
Buried DeSoto at night beneath the Mississippi.

Little Crow died with skunk-fur bands on his wrists.
Long Head charged the rifles naked. Some men
Taunted the Algonquins while tied to the stake.
Others died on high scaffolds in Texas;
Hat Sutton died in Great Neck on a rope.
MacKenzie broke up on the Labrador rocks.
These risky ones died in ambushes, in dance
Halls, with cow skulls in the Snake River snows.

A soldier wrote to his mother: "Today we marched
Back, after a battle, to our previous position
In a heavy rain. We passed a drunk man
Asleep in the ditch. It was General Grant."
All the old singing says it: It will all
End in ashes. The kept life is the lost life.
It is still true. What moves us in our tents?
The spectacle of Grant, lying drunk, in the rain.

II
SILENCE IN THE
SNOWY FIELDS
and Related Poems
1958–78

Waiting for Night to Come

I

How much I long for the night to come
Again—I am restless all afternoon—
And the huge stars to appear
All over the heavens! . . . The black spaces between
     stars . . .
And the blue to fade away.

II

I worked on poems with my back to the window,
Waiting for the darkness that I remember
Noticing from my cradle.
When I step over and open the door, I am
A salmon slipping over the gravel into the ocean.

III

One star stands alone in the western darkness:
Arcturus. Caught in their love, the Arabs called it
The Keeper of Heaven. I think
It was in the womb that I received
The thirst for the dark heavens.

Night

I

If I think of a horse wandering about sleeplessly
All night on this short grass covered with moonlight,
I feel a joy, as if I had thought
Of a pirate ship ploughing through dark flowers.

II

The box elders around us are full of joy,
Obeying what is beneath them.
The lilacs are sleeping, and the plants are sleeping;
Even the wood made into a casket is asleep.

III

The butterfly is carrying loam on its wings;
The toad is bearing tiny bits of granite in his skin.
The leaves at the crown of the tree are asleep
Like the dark bits of earth at its root.

IV

Alive, we are like a sleek black water beetle,
Skating across still water in any direction
We choose, and soon to be swallowed
Suddenly from beneath.

SNOWFALL IN THE AFTERNOON

I

The grass is half-covered with snow.
It was the sort of snowfall that starts in late afternoon,
And now the little houses of the grass are growing
    dark.

II

If I could reach down, near the earth,
I could take handfuls of darkness!
A darkness that was always there, which we never
    noticed.

III

As the snow grows heavier, the cornstalks fade farther
    away,
And the barn moves nearer to the house.
The barn moves all alone in the growing storm.

IV

The barn is full of corn, and moving toward us now,
Like a hulk blown toward us in a storm at sea;
All the sailors on deck have been blind for many
    years.

A PRIVATE FALL

Motes of haydust rise and fall
With slow and grave steps,
Like servants who dance in the yard
Because some prince has been born.

What has been born? The winter.
Then the Egyptians were right.
Everything wants a chance to die,
To begin in the clear fall air.

Each leaf sinks and goes down
When we least expect it.
We glance toward the window for some-
Thing has caught our eye.

It's possible autumn is a tomb
Out of which a child is born.
We feel a secret joy
And we tell no one!

Late at Night During a Visit of Friends

I

We spent all day fishing and talking.
At last, late at night, I sit at my desk alone,
And rise and walk out in the summery night.
A dark thing hopped near me in the grass.

II

The trees were breathing, the windmill slowly
    pumped.
Overhead the rain clouds that rained on Ortonville
Covered half the stars.
The air was still cool from their rain.

III

It is very late.
I am the only one awake.
Men and women I love are sleeping nearby.

IV

The human face shines as it speaks of things
Near itself, thoughts full of dreams.
The human face shines like a dark sky
As it speaks of those things that oppress the living.

OLD BOARDS

I

I love to see boards lying on the ground in early
     spring:
The ground beneath them is wet and muddy—
Perhaps covered with chicken tracks—
And they are dry and eternal.

II

This is the wood one sees on the decks of ocean ships,
Wood that carries us far from land,
With a dryness of something used for simple tasks,
Like a horse's tail.

III

This wood is like a man who has a simple life,
Living through the spring and winter on the ship of
     his own desire.
He sits on dry wood surrounded by half-melted snow
As the rooster walks away springily over the
     dampened hay.

SOLITUDE LATE AT NIGHT IN THE WOODS

I

The body is like a November birch facing the full
   moon
And reaching into the cold heavens.
In these trees there is no ambition, no sodden body,
   no leaves,
Nothing but bare trunks climbing like cold fire!

II

My last walk in the trees has come. At dawn
I must return to the trapped fields,
To the obedient earth.
The trees shall be reaching all the winter.

III

It is a joy to walk in the bare woods.
The moonlight is not broken by the heavy leaves.
The leaves are down, and touching the soaked earth,
Giving off the odor that partridges love.

Surprised by Evening

There is unknown dust that is near us,
Waves breaking on shores just over the hill,
Trees full of birds that we have never seen,
Nets drawn down with dark fish.

The evening arrives; we look up and it is there,
It has come through the nets of the stars,
Through the tissues of the grass,
Walking quietly over the asylums of the waters.

The day shall never end, we think:
We have hair that seems born for the daylight;
But, at last, the quiet waters of the night will rise,
And our skin shall see far off, as it does underwater.

Three Kinds of Pleasures

I

Sometimes, riding in a car, in Wisconsin
Or Illinois, you notice those dark telephone poles
One by one lift themselves out of the fence line
And slowly leap on the gray sky—
And past them, the snowy fields.

II

The darkness drifts down like snow on the picked
    cornfields
In Wisconsin: and on these black trees
Scattered, one by one,
Through the winter fields—
We see stiff weeds and brownish stubble,
And white snow left now only in the wheeltracks of
    the combine.

III

It is a pleasure, also, to be driving
Toward Chicago, near dark,
And see the lights in the barns.
The bare trees more dignified than ever,
Like a fierce man on his deathbed,
And the ditches along the road half full of a private
    snow.

THE CALL AWAY

A cold wind flows over the cornfields;
Fleets of blackbirds ride that ocean.
I want to be in that wild, be
Outdoors, live anywhere in the wind.

I settle down, with my back against
A shed wall where no one can find me.
I stare out at the box elder leaves
Moving in this mysterious water.

What is it that I want? Not money,
Not a large desk, a house with ten rooms.
This is what I want to do: To sit here,
Take no part, be called away by wind.

After Drinking All Night with a Friend, We Go Out in a Boat at Dawn to See Who Can Write the Best Poem

These pines, these fall oaks, these rocks,
This water dark and touched by wind—
I am like you, you dark boat,
Drifting over water fed by cool springs.

Beneath the waters, since I was a boy,
I have dreamt of strange and dark treasures,
Not of gold or strange stones, but the true
Gift, beneath the pale lakes of Minnesota.

This morning also, drifting in the dawn wind,
I sense my hands, and my shoes, and this ink—
Drifting, as all of the body drifts,
Above the clouds of the flesh and the stone.

A few friendships, a few dawns, a few glimpses of
    grass,
A few oars weathered by the snow and the heat,
So we drift toward shore, over cold waters,
No longer caring if we drift or go straight.

POEM IN THREE PARTS

I

Oh, on an early morning I think I shall live forever!
I am wrapped in my joyful flesh,
As the grass is wrapped in its clouds of green.

II

Rising from a bed, where I dreamt
Of long rides past castles and hot coals,
The sun lies happily on my knees;
I have suffered and survived the night
Bathed in dark water, like any blade of grass.

III

The strong leaves of the box elder tree,
Plunging in the wind, call us to disappear
Into the wilds of the universe,
Where we shall sit at the foot of a plant,
And live forever, like the dust.

WATERING THE HORSE

How strange to think of giving up all ambition!
Suddenly I see with such clear eyes
The white flake of snow
That has just fallen in the horse's mane!

Driving to Town Late to Mail a Letter

It is a cold and snowy night. The main street is deserted.
The only things moving are swirls of snow.
As I lift the mailbox door, I feel its cold iron.
There is a privacy I love in this snowy night.
Driving around, I will waste more time.

Waking from Sleep

Inside the veins there are navies setting forth,
Tiny explosions at the waterlines,
And seagulls weaving in the wind of the salty blood.

It is the morning. The country has slept the whole
  winter.
Window seats are covered with fur skins, the yard is
  full
Of stiff dogs, and hands that clumsily hold heavy
  books.

Now we wake, and rise from bed, and eat
  breakfast!—
Shouts rise from the harbor of the blood,
Mist, and masts rising, the knocks of wooden tackle in
  the sunlight.

Now we sing, and do tiny dances on the kitchen floor.
Our whole body is like a harbor at dawn;
We know that our master has left us for the day.

DRIVING TOWARD THE LAC QUI PARLE RIVER

I

I am driving; it is dusk; Minnesota.
The stubble field catches the last growth of sun.
The soybeans are breathing on all sides.
Old men are sitting before their houses on car seats
In the small towns. I am happy,
The moon rising above the turkey sheds.

II

The small world of the car
Plunges through the deep fields of the night,
On the road from Willmar to Milan.
This solitude covered with iron
Moves through the fields of night
Penetrated by the noise of crickets.

III

Nearly to Milan, suddenly a small bridge,
And water kneeling in the moonlight.
In small towns the houses are built right on the
    ground;
The lamplight falls on all fours in the grass.
When I reach the river, the full moon covers it;
A few people are talking low in a boat.

Love Poem

When we are in love, we love the grass,
And the barns, and the light poles,
And the small main streets abandoned all night.

"Taking the Hands"

Taking the hands of someone you love,
You see they are delicate cages . . .
Tiny birds are singing
In the secluded prairies
And in the deep valleys of the hands.

First Snowfall

The snow begins falling.
A winter of privacy is before us,
Winter privacy,
The vast halls inside the heads of animals
Lie before us, the slow
Breaking of day, warm blood moving, moving,
And immense pine trees.

After Working

I

After many strange thoughts,
Thoughts of distant harbors, and new life,
I came in and found the moonlight lying on the floor.

II

Outside it covers the trees like pure sound,
The sound of tower bells, or of water moving under
    the ice,
The sound of the deaf hearing through the bones of
    their heads.

III

We know the road; as the moonlight
Lifts everything, so in a night like this
The road goes on ahead; it is all clear.

A Man Writes to a Part of Himself

What cave are you in, hiding, rained on?
Like a wife, starving, without care,
Water dripping from your head, bent
Over ground corn. . . .

　　You raise your face into the rain
That drives across the valley.
Forgive me, your husband,
On the streets of a distant city, laughing,
With many appointments,
Though at night going also
To a bare room, a room of poverty,
To sleep beside a bare pitcher and basin
In a room with no heat—

　　Which of us two then is the worse off?
And how did this separation come about?

Depression

I felt my heart beat like an engine high in the air,
Like those scaffolding engines standing only on
    planks;
My body hung about me like an old grain elevator,
Useless, clogged, full of blackened wheat.
My body was sour, my life dishonest, and I fell asleep.

I dreamt that men came toward me, carrying thin
    wires;
The wires, like fire, passed in; the men were old
    Tibetans,
Dressed in padded clothes, to keep out cold;
Then three work gloves, lying fingers to fingers,
In a circle, came toward me, and I awoke.

What does the dream say? It says that I am
A liar; that I am not a true man. Now
I want to see nothing more than two feet high.
I want to meet no one; I want to say nothing;
I want to go down and rest in the black earth of
    silence.

THE MANSION

Some people are ready
To die now, like
This pigeon-grass clump
That dies so quietly.

I am not, and yet
Today I saw crushed oyster
Shells on the ground,
Like doors into the earth

Made of mother-of-pearl,
Thin slivers of glass,
A white chicken's feather
That still seems excited

By the warm blood,
And an empty corn-
Cob on the ground beside
Them, so beautiful!

Room after room,
Mansion after
Mansion in its empty
Rosy house.

After Long Busyness

I start out for a walk at last after weeks at the desk.
Moon gone, plowing underfoot, no stars; not a trace
    of light!
Suppose a horse were galloping toward me in this
    open field?
Every day I did not spend in solitude was wasted.

The Moon

After writing poems all day,
I go off to see the moon in the pines.
Far in the woods I sit down against a pine.
The moon has her porches turned to face the light,
But the deep part of her house is in darkness.

THINKING OF TU FU'S POEM

I get up late and ask what has to be done today.
Nothing has to be done, so the farm looks doubly
    good.
The blowing maple leaves fit so well with the moving
    grass,
The shadow of my writing shack looks small beside
    the growing trees.

Never be with your children, let them get stringy like
    radishes!
Let your wife worry about the lack of money!
Your whole life is like a drunkard's dream!
You haven't combed your hair for a whole month!

AFTER SPENDING A WEEK ALONE

After writing for a week alone in my old shack,
I guide the car through Ortonville around midnight.

The policeman talks intently in his swivel chair.
And the ceiling light shines on his bald head.

Soon the car picks up speed again beside the quarries.
The moonspot on the steel tracks moves so fast!

Thirty or so Black Angus hold down their earth
Among silvery grasses blown back and forth in the
    wind.

My family is still away, no one at home.
How sweet it is to come back to an empty house—

The windows dark, no lamps lit, trees still,
The barn serious and mature in the moonlight.

WINTER PRIVACY POEMS AT THE SHACK

I

About four, a few flakes.
I empty the teapot out in the snow,
Feeling shoots of joy in the new cold.
By nightfall, wind;
The curtains on the south sway softly.

II

My shack has two rooms; I use one.
The lamplight falls on my chair and table,
And I fly into one of my own poems—
I can't tell you where—
As if I appeared where I am now,
In a wet field, snow falling.

III

More of the fathers are dying each day.
It is time for the sons.
Bits of darkness are gathering around them.
The darkness appears as flakes of light.

IV

Listening to Bach's Cello Concerto

Inside this music there is someone
Who is not well described
By the names of Jesus, or Jehovah, or the Lord of
    Hosts.

V

There is a solitude like black mud!
Sitting in the darkness singing,
I can't tell if this joy
Is from the body, or the soul, or a third place!

VI

When I wake, new snow has fallen.
I am alone, yet someone else is with me,
Drinking coffee, looking out at the snow.

Moses's Basket

I don't know if we love most the divine
Or the human. The Pharaoh's wife at dawn—
Do you remember?—wades out into the reeds.
The baby and the Pharaoh are about to meet.

Moses's basket floated on Red Sea water.
And the reeds, weren't they beautifully delicate,
Alluvial, bird-filled, and marshy . . .
The sweet hair of the Water Mother?

They were. We cherish nothing more than the reeds.
But it is the basket with the baby in it,
Rocking in darkening reeds, that our eyes love to see,
And the curving lines the basket makes in the river
    water.

Passing an Orchard by Train

Grass high under apple trees.
The bark of the trees rough and sexual,
The grass growing heavy and uneven.

We cannot bear disaster, like
The rocks—
Swaying nakedly
In open fields.

One slight bruise and we die!
I know no one on this train.
A man comes walking down the aisle.
I want to tell him
That I forgive him, that I want him
To forgive me.

III
THE LIGHT AROUND
THE BODY

and Related Poems
1957–70

But when this had given me many a hard blow, doubtless from the Spirit that had a desire for me, I finally fell into great sadness and melancholy, when I viewed the great depth of this world, the sun and the stars and the clouds, rain and snow, and contemplated in my mind the whole creation of this world.

So then I found in all things good and evil, love and wrath, in creatures of reason as well as in wood, in stone, in earth, in the elements, in men and animals. Withal, I considered the little spark "man" and what it might be esteemed to be by God in comparison with this great work of heaven and earth.

In consequence I grew very melancholy, and what is written, though I knew it well, could not console me.

—Jacob Boehme

What a distressing contrast there is between the radiant intelligence of the child and the feeble mentality of the average adult.

—Freud

O dear children, look in what a dungeon we are lying, in what lodging we are, for we have been captured by the spirit of the outward world; it is our life, for it nourishes and brings us up, it rules in our marrow and bones, in our flesh and blood, it has made our flesh earthly, and now death has us.

—Jacob Boehme

CONFUSIONS

1

Here Morgan dies like a dog among whispers of
    angels;
The saint is born among tin cans in the orchard;
A rose receives the name of "The General Jackson."
Here snow-white blossoms bloom in the bare homes
Of bankmen, and with a lily the Pope meets
A delegation of waves, and blesses the associations
Of the ocean; I walk with a coarse body through
    winds
That carry the birds on their long roads to the poles,
And see the ghost of Locke above the railroad tracks.

2

A bitterness ascends from the Gulf, and fights
Its way up the Mississippi; no one knows
What to do. Andrew Jackson and two friends
Put on Roman togas, and sit up all night
Speaking Latin in a log house in Tennessee.
And women in sod huts, beneath horse blankets,
Something stifling, something wee, something living
    in a well—
Something living in a wall, forgotten, my grandfather
Driving horses along the slats of the plaster—

3

Mesopotamian scrolls fall off a wagon in New York;
Ground up, they end mingling with the snow drifting
Against the door of a pighouse in Montana.
Salesmen in small Missouri and Kansas towns
Enter Masonic halls, put on turbans,
And ask for money to rebuild the Second Temple.
As we lift a glass of water to swallow it
We see at the bottom the boards Geronimo
Found under his bed in Florida when he awoke.

Winter Afternoon in Greenwich Village

It is Sunday afternoon. The shadows seem so
  frightening
On the brownstone sills. The Missouri River must be
  flowing
The same muddy brown! The bullboats cross the
  river
Silently in the naked moonlight. I cannot say
Why a Sunday afternoon in a New York apartment
Should seem to be night among the teepees at Jackson
  Hole.
Jim Bridger lugs his Shakespeare through the stumps;
In his shack, he swears at Iago far into the night.
Outdoors a beaver swims in the mountain stream,
Feeling with his nose the door of his home like a
  beehive,
Moving in a darkness the color of Indian hair.
The tips of the small willows move above the silent
  water.

CALLING TO THE BADGER

Come, let us write of Niagara and the Huron squaws,
The Puritans with their black robes, Dillinger
Like a dark wind. Bring in the advertising men,
So that the strong-haunched woman
By the blazing stove of the sun, the moon,
May come home to us, sitting on the naked wood
In another world, and all the Shell stations folded in a
    faint light.

Come, let us write of the sadness of the Indian
    fighters,
The sadness that rises from the death of the Diggers,
From the death of Logan alone in his house,
And the Cherokees forced to eat the tail of the Great
    Bear.
The old are being driven to Florida
Like Geronimo, and young men are still calling to the
    badger
And the otter, alone on the mountains of South
    Dakota.

SLEET STORM ON THE MERRITT PARKWAY

I look out at the white sleet covering the still streets
As we drive through Scarsdale—
The sleet began falling as we left Connecticut,
And in the wet air after cars winter leaves swirled
Like hands suddenly turned over in a conversation.
Now the frost has nearly buried the short grass of
    March.
Seeing the sheets of sleet untouched on the wide streets,
I think of the many comfortable homes stretching for
    miles,
Two and three stories, solid, with polished floors,
With white curtains in the upstairs bedrooms,
And small perfume flagons of black glass on the
    windowsills,
And warm bathrooms with guest towels, and electric
    lights—
What a magnificent place for a child to grow up!
And yet the children end in the river of price-fixing,
Or in the snowy field of the insane asylum.
The sleet falls—so many cars moving toward New
    York—
Last night we argued about the Marines invading
    Guatemala in 1947.
The United Fruit Company had one water spigot for
    200 families;
We talked about the ideals of America,
The slave systems of Rome and Greece, and no one
    agreed.

MELANCHOLIA

1

A light seen suddenly in the storm, snow
Coming from all sides, like flakes
Of sleep, and myself
On the road to the dark barn,
Halfway there, a black dog near me.

2

Light on the wooden rail.
Someone I knew and loved.
As we hear the dates of his marriage
And the years he moved,
A wreath of dark fir and shiny laurel
Slips off the coffin.

3

A cathedral: I see
Starving men, weakened, leaning
On their knees. But the bells ring anyway,
Sending out over the planted fields
A vegetation, sound waves with long leaves.

4

There is a wound on the trunk,
Where the branch was torn off.
A wind comes out of it,
Rising, swelling,
Swirling over everything alive.

Three Presidents

Andrew Jackson

I want to be a white horse!
I want to be a white horse on the green mountains!
A horse that runs over wooden bridges and sleeps
In abandoned barns. . . .

Theodore Roosevelt

When I was President, I crushed snails with my bare
    teeth.
I slept in my underwear in the White House.
I ate the Cubans with a straw, and Lenin dreamt of
    me every night.
I wore down a forest of willow trees. I ground the
    snow,
And sold it.
The mountains of Texas shall heal our cornfields,
Overrun by the yellow race.
As for me, I want to be a stone! Yes!
I want to be a stone laid down thousands of years ago,
A stone with almost invisible cracks!
I want to be a stone that holds up the edge of the lake
    house,
A stone that suddenly gets up and runs around at
    night,
And lets the marriage bed fall; a stone that leaps into
    the water,
Carrying the robber down with him.

John F. Kennedy

I want to be a stream of water falling—
Water falling from high in the mountains, water
That dissolves everything,
And is never drunk, falling from ledge to ledge, from
    glass to glass.
I want the air around me to be invisible, resilient,
Able to flow past rocks.
I will carry the boulders with me to the valley.
Then ascending I will fall through space again:
Glittering in the sun, like the crystal in sideboards,
Goblets of the old life, before it was ruined by the
    Church.
And when I ascend the third time, I will fall forever,
Missing the earth entirely.

THE EXECUTIVE'S DEATH

Merchants have multiplied more than the stars of
    heaven.
Half the population are like the long grasshoppers
That sleep in the bushes in the cool of the day:
The sound of their wings is heard at noon, muffled,
    near the earth.
The crane handler dies, the taxi driver dies, slumped
    over
In his taxi. Meanwhile, high in the air, an executive
Walks on the cool floor, and suddenly falls.
He dreams he is lost in a snowstorm in a mountain,
On which he crashed, carried at night by great
    machines.
As he lies on the wintery slope, cut off and dying,
A pine stump talks to him of Goethe and Jesus.
Commuters arrive in Hartford at dusk like moles
Or hares flying from a fire behind them,
And the dusk in Hartford is full of their sighs;
Their trains come through the air like a dark music,
Like the sound of horns, the sound of thousands of
    small wings.

SMOTHERED BY THE WORLD

Chrysanthemums crying out on the borders of death,
Lone teeth walking in the icy waters,
Once more the heavy body mourns!
It howls outside the hedges of life,
Pushed out of the enclosure.
Now it must meet the death outside the death.
Living outside the gate is one death,
Cold faces gather along the wall,
A bag of bones warms itself in a tree.
Long and bitter antlers sway in the dark,
The hairy tail howls in the dirt . . .

COME WITH ME

Come with me into those things that have felt this
    despair for so long—
Those removed Chevrolet wheels that howl with a
    terrible loneliness,
Lying on their backs in the cindery dirt, like men
    drunk and naked,
Staggering off down a hill at night to drown at last in
    a pond.
Those shredded inner tubes abandoned on the
    shoulders of thruways,
Black and collapsed bodies, that tried and burst, and
    were left behind.
And those curly steel shavings, scattered about on
    garage benches,
Sometimes still warm, gritty when we hold them,
Who have given up and blame everything on the
    government;
And those roads in South Dakota that feel around in
    the darkness. . . .

A Pint of Whisky and Five Cigars

1

If we go back, if we walk into the old darkness,
We will find Washington brooding under the long
    bridges,
Jefferson weeping, and the cries of Indians
Echoing in the compression chambers of shells.

2

The Choctaws were told to hold the shells to their
    ears
And pretend they could hear the far-off sea.
We all knew what was at stake; both
The Europeans and the Sioux wanted holy ground.

3

You have seen them, holders of hardware stores
And the richest mayors: something immensely old
Comes up behind them, and they disappear into it
And lose their place on the dancing floor.

4

I had a granduncle who was a horse beater,
And was knocked down once by a horse and bitten.
When he lost his farms, his wife rationed him
To a pint of whisky and five cigars a day.

THOSE BEING EATEN BY AMERICA

The cry of those being eaten by America,
Others pale and soft being stored for later eating

And Jefferson
Who saw hope in new oats

The wild houses go on
With long hair growing from between their toes
The feet at night get up
And run down the long white roads by themselves

The dams reverse themselves and want to go stand
    alone in the desert

Ministers who dive headfirst into the earth
The pale flesh
Spreading guiltily into new literatures

That is why these poems are so sad
The long dead running over the fields

The mass sinking down
The light in children's faces fading at six or seven

The world will soon break up into small colonies of
    the saved

WRITTEN IN DEJECTION NEAR ROME

What if these long races go on repeating themselves
Century after century, living in houses painted light
    colors
On the beach,
Black spiders,
Having turned pale and fat,
Men walking thoughtfully with their families,
Vibrations
Of exhausted violin-bodies,
Horrible eternities of sea pines!
Some men cannot help but feel it,
They will abandon their homes
To live on rafts tied together on the ocean;
Those on shore will go inside tree trunks,
Surrounded by bankers whose fingers have grown
    long and slender,
Piercing through rotting bark for their food.

MAX ERNST AND THE TORTOISE'S BEAK

1

Floating in turtle blood, going backward and forward,
We wake up like a mad sea urchin
On the bloody fields near the secret pass—
There the dead sleep in jars. . . .

2

Or we got at night slowly into the tunnels of the
    tortoise's claws,
Carrying chunks of the moon
To light the tunnels,
Listening for the sound of rocks falling into the sea, . . .

3

Waking, we find ourselves in the tortoise's beak,
As he carries us high
Over New Jersey—going swiftly
Through the darkness between the constellations. . . .

4

At dawn we are still transparent, pulling
In the starlight; high up near the stars,
We are still falling like a room
Full of moonlight through the air. . . .

EVOLUTION FROM THE FISH

This grandson of fishes holds inside him
A hundred thousand small black stones.
This nephew of snails, six feet long, lies naked on a
    bed
With a smiling woman. His head throws off light
Under marble; he is moving toward his own life
Like fur, walking. And when the frost comes, he is
Fur, mammoth fur, growing longer
And silkier, passing the woman's dormitory,
Kissing a stomach, leaning against a pillar,
He moves toward the animal, the animal with furry
    head!

What a joy to smell the flesh of a new child!
Like new grass! And this long man with the student
    girl,
Coffee cups, her pale waist, the spirit moving around
    them,
Moves, dragging a great tail into the darkness.
In the night we blaze up, drawing pictures
Of spiny fish; we throw off the white stones!
Serpents rise from the ocean floor with spiral
    motions;
A man goes inside a jewel, and sleeps. Do
Not hold my hands down! Let me raise them!
A fire is passing up through the soles of my feet!

Looking into a Face

Conversation brings us so close! Opening
The surfs of the body,
Bringing fish up near the sun,
And stiffening the backbones of the sea!

I have wandered in a face, for hours,
Passing through dark fires.
I have risen to a body
Not yet born,
Existing like a light around the body,
Through which the body moves like a sliding moon.

A Month of Happiness

A blind horse stands among cherry trees.
And bones shine from cool earth.
The heart leaps
Almost up to the sky! But laments
And filaments pull us back into the dark.
Night takes us. But
A paw
Comes out of the dark
To light the road. I'll be all right.
I follow my own fiery traces through the night.

THE CELTIC CHURCH

An owl on the dark waters.
And torches smoking
By mossy stone.
The horse gallops through the night.
A candle flutters as a black hand
Reaches out toward it.

All of these images mean
A man with coins on his eyes,
And the vast waters,
The cry of seagulls.

OPENING AN OYSTER ON RUE JACOB

For Max Ernst

We think of Charlemagne
As we open oysters.
Looking down, we see
Crowds waving from islands inside the oyster shell.
The neck swings to bite the dog.
When the fishermen take in their floats
They lift nets some giant fish
Broke through at night.
At dusk we start north with twenty dogs.
Blowing snow
Makes us lower our heads
And miles of snow crust
Go past between the runners!
The Arctic plains are an immense maternity hospital
Turned white by oyster shells!
But in the director's office there is a pebble
That has drawn in
The malignancy of the shark. . . .
And a mammoth hair
That can melt an entire Russian county,
Drowning chickens and cows—then we know
That if we climb into an attic in Kansas
We will find the rumpled cloth
That a minister held over the faces of the two young
    kings!

ROMANS ANGRY ABOUT THE INNER WORLD

What shall the world do with its children?
At sixteen we have experiences
The old men know nothing of—
A leaping of the body—
The body rolling—I have felt it—
And we float
Joyfully on the dark places.
But the executioners
Move toward Drusia.
They tie her legs
On the iron horse: "Here is a woman
Who has caught a glimpse of Our Mother
In the other world!" Next they warm
The hooks. The Romans had put their trust
In iron. Irons glowed
Like teeth. They asked her
To assure them. She refused. Finally
They took burning
Pine sticks, and pushed them
Into her side. Her breath rose
And she died. The executioners
Rolled her off onto the ground.
Snow fell from the clear sky,
Covering the naked and mangled body,
And the executioners, astonished, withdrew.

Drusia's joy is like a thorn
In the ear of a tiny beast.

Our fingers are too thick
To pull it out.
That joy is like a jagged stone
Flying toward us out of the dark.

AS THE ASIAN WAR BEGINS

There are longings to kill that cannot be seen,
Or are seen only by a minister who no longer believes
      in God,
Living in his parish like a crow in its nest.

And there are flowers with murky centers,
Impenetrable, ebony, basalt . . .

Conestogas go past, over the Platte, their contents
Hidden from us, murderers riding under the canvas . . .

Give us a glimpse of what we cannot see,
Our enemies, the soldiers and the poor.

COUNTING SMALL-BONED BODIES

Let's count the bodies over again.

If we could only make the bodies smaller,
The size of skulls,
We could make a whole plain white with skulls in the
    moonlight!

If we could only make the bodies smaller,
Maybe we could get
A year's kill in front of us on a desk!

If we could only make the bodies smaller,
We could fit
A body into a finger-ring, for a keepsake forever.

HATRED OF MEN WITH BLACK HAIR

I hear voices praising Tshombe, and the Portuguese
In Angola, these are the men who skinned Little Crow!
We are all their sons, skulking
In back rooms, selling nails with trembling hands!

We distrust every person on earth with black hair;
We send teams to overthrow Chief Joseph's
     government;
We train natives to kill Presidents with blow darts;
We have men loosening the nails on Noah's ark.

The State Department floats in the heavy jellies near
     the bottom
Like exhausted crustaceans, like squids who are
     confused,
Sending out beams of black light to the open sea,
Fighting their fraternal feeling for the great landlords.

We have violet rays that light up the jungles at night,
     showing
The friendly populations; we are teaching the children
     of ritual
To overcome their longing for life, and we send
Sparks of black light that fit the holes in the generals' eyes.

Underneath all the cement of the Pentagon
There is a drop of Indian blood preserved in snow:
Preserved from the trail of blood that once led away
From the stockade, over the snow, the trail now lost.

Johnson's Cabinet Watched by Ants

1

It is a clearing deep in a forest: overhanging boughs
Make a low place. Here citizens we know during the
    day,
The ministers, the department heads,
Appear changed: the stockholders of large steel
    companies
In small wooden shoes. Here are the generals dressed
    as gamboling lambs.

2

Tonight they burn the rice supplies; tomorrow
They lecture on Thoreau; tonight they move around
    the trees,
Tomorrow they pick the twigs from their clothes;
Tonight they throw the firebombs, tomorrow
They read the Declaration of Independence;
    tomorrow they are in church.

3

Ants are gathered around an old tree.
In a choir they sing, in harsh and gravelly voices,
Old Etruscan songs on tyranny.
Toads nearby clap their small hands, and join
The fiery songs, their five long toes trembling in the
    soaked earth.

AFTER THE INDUSTRIAL REVOLUTION, ALL THINGS HAPPEN AT ONCE

Now we enter a strange world, where the Hessian
    Christmas
Still goes on, and Washington has not reached the
    other shore;
The Whiskey Boys
Are gathering again on the meadows of Pennsylvania
And the Republic is still sailing on the open sea.

I saw a black angel in Washington dancing
On a barge, saying, "Let us now divide kennel dogs
And hunting dogs"; Henry Cabot Lodge, in New
    York,
Talking of sugarcane in Cuba; Ford,
In Detroit, drinking mother's milk;
Henry Cabot Lodge, saying, "Remember the *Maine*!"
Ford, saying, "History is bunk!"
And Wilson saying, "What is good for General
    Motors . . . "

Who is it, singing? Don't you hear singing?
It is the dead of Cripple Creek;
Coxey's army
Like turkeys are singing from the tops of trees!
And the Whiskey Boys are drunk outside
    Philadelphia.

Hurrying Away From the Earth

The poor and the dazed and the idiots
Are with us, they live in the casket of the sun
And the moon's coffin, as I walk out tonight
Seeing the night wheel its dark wheelbarrow
All about the plains of heaven,
And the stars inexorably rising.
Dark moon! Sinister tears!
Shadows of slums and of the conquering dead!

One man pierced his chest with a long needle
To stop his heart from beating anymore.
Another put blocks of ice in his bed
So he would die; a woman
Washed her hair, and hanged herself
In the long braids. Climbing a high
Elm above her lawn, another
Opened a box, and swallowed poisonous spiders.

The time for exhortation is past. I have heard
The iron chairs scraping in the Newark asylum,
In November, as the cold bird
Hunches into the windy nights of winter.
Coal miners rise from their pits
Like a flash flood, like a wall disintegrating.
A forty-year-old man breaks into tears
When he hears that someone has risen from the dead.

IV
THE TEETH MOTHER
NAKED AT LAST
1970-72

The Teeth Mother Naked at Last

Massive engines lift beautifully from the deck.
Wings appear over the trees, wings with eight
    hundred rivets.

Engines burning a thousand gallons of gasoline a
    minute sweep over the huts with dirt floors.

The chickens feel the new fear deep in the pits of
    their beaks.
Buddha with Padma Sambhava.

Meanwhile, out on the China Sea,
Immense gray bodies are floating,
Born in Roanoke,
The ocean on both sides expanding, "buoyed on the
    dense marine."

Helicopters flutter overhead. The death-
Bee is coming. Super Sabres
Like knots of neurotic energy sweep
Around and return.
This is Hamilton's triumph.
This is the advantage of a centralized bank.
B–52s come from Guam. All the teachers
Die in flames. The hopes of Tolstoy fall asleep in the
    ant heap.
Do not ask for mercy.

Now the time comes to look into the past-tunnels,
The hours given and taken in school,
The scuffles in coatrooms,
Foam leaps from his nostrils,
Now we come to the scum you take from the mouths
　　of the dead,
Now we sit beside the dying, and hold their hands;
　　there is hardly time for good-bye.
The staff sergeant from North Carolina is dying—
　　you hold his hand,
He knows the mansions of the dead are empty, he has
　　an empty place
Inside him, created one night when his parents came
　　home drunk.
He uses half his skin to cover it,
As you try to protect a balloon from sharp objects. . . .

Artillery shells explode. Napalm canisters roll end
　　over end.
800 steel pellets fly through the vegetable walls.
The six-hour infant puts his fists instinctively to his
　　eyes to keep out the light.
But the room explodes;
The children explode;
Blood leaps on the vegetable walls.

Yes, I know, blood leaps on the walls—
Don't cry at that—
Do you cry at the wind pouring out of Canada?

Do you cry at the reeds shaken at the edge of the
   sloughs?
The Marine battalion enters.
This happens when the seasons change,
This happens when the leaves begin to drop from the
   trees too early
"Kill them: I don't want to see anything moving."
This happens when the ice begins to show its teeth in
   the ponds.
This happens when the heavy layers of lake water
   press down on the fish's head, and send him
   deeper, where his tail swirls slowly, and his brain
   passes him pictures of heavy reeds, of vegetation
   fall on vegetation. . . .

2

Excellent Roman knives slip along the ribs.

A stronger man starts to jerk up the strips of flesh.

*"Let's hear it again, you believe in the Father, the Son,
   and the Holy Ghost?"*

A long scream unrolls.

More.

*"From the political point of view, democratic
   institutions are being built in Vietnam, wouldn't
   you agree?"*

A green parrot shudders under the fingernails.
Blood jumps in the pocket.
The scream lashes like a tail.
"Let us not be deterred from our task by the voices of
dissent. . . ."

The whines of the jets
Pierce like a long needle.

3

It is a desire to eat death,
To gobble it down,
To rush on it like a cobra with mouth open.
It is a desire to take death inside,
To feel it burning inside, pushing out velvety hairs,
Like a clothes brush in the intestines—

That is the thrill that leads the President on to lie.

Now the Chief Executive enters, and the press
    conference begins.
First the President lies about the date the Appalachian
    Mountains rose.
Then he lies about the population of Chicago.
Then the number of fish taken every year in the
    Arctic,
Then about the weight of the adult eagle, then about
    the acreage of the Everglades.
He has learned the true birthplace of Attila the Hun,

Then he lies about the composition of the amniotic
    fluid.
He has private information about which city *is* the
    capital of Wyoming.

He insists that Luther was never a German,
And declares that only the Protestants sold
    indulgences,
That Pope Leo X *wanted* to reform the Church, but
    the liberal elements prevented him.
That the Peasant's War was fomented by Italians from
    the North.
And the Attorney General lies about the time the sun
    sets.

4

These lies mean we have a longing to die.
What is there now to hold us on earth?
It is the longing for someone to come and take us by
    the hand to where they are all sleeping:
Where the Egyptian pharaohs are asleep, and our own
    mothers,
And all those disappeared children, who went around
    with us on the rings at grade school.

Do not be angry at the President—
He is longing to take in his hands the locks of death-
    hair:
To meet his own children, dead, or never born. . . .

* * *

He is drifting sideways toward the dusty places.

5

This is what it's like to watch the altimeter needle
    going mad

*Baron 25, this is 81. Are there any friendlies in the
    area? 81 from 25, negative on the friendlies. I'd
    like you to take out as many structures as possible
    located in those trees within 200 meters east and
    west of my smoke mark.*

diving, the green earth swinging, cheeks hanging back,
    red pins blossoming ahead of us, 20-millimeter
    cannon fire, leveling off, rice fields shooting by
    like telephone poles, smoke rising, hut roofs loom
    up huge as landing fields, slugs going in, half the
    huts on fire, small figures running, palm trees
    burning, shooting past, up again; . . . blue sky . . .
    cloud mountains . . .

This is what it's like to have a gross national product.

It is because we have so few women sobbing in back
    rooms,
Because we have so few children's heads torn apart by
    high-velocity bullets,
Because we have so few tears falling on our own hands

That the Super Sabre turns and screams down toward
    the earth.

6

A car is rolling toward a rock wall.
The treads in the face begin to crack.
We feel like tires being run down roads under heavy
    cars.

The teenager imagines herself floating through the
    Seven Spheres.
Oven doors are found
Open.
Soot collects over the door frame, has children, takes
    courses, goes mad, and dies.

There is a black silo inside our bodies.
Bits of black paint are flaking off,
Where the motorcycles roar, around and around,
Rising higher on the silo walls,
The bodies bent toward the horizon,
Driven by angry women dressed in black.

7

I know that books are tired of us.
I know they are chaining the Bible to chairs.
Books don't want to remain in the same room with us
    anymore.

New Testaments are escaping . . . dressed as women . . .
    they slip out after dark.
And Plato! Plato . . . Plato
Wants to hurry back up the river of time,
So he can end as a blob of seaflesh rotting on an
    Australian beach.

8

Why are they dying? I have written this so many
    times.
They are dying because the President has opened a
    Bible again.
They are dying because gold deposits have been
    found among the Shoshoni Indians.
They are dying because money follows intellect,
And intellect is like a fan opening in the wind.

The Marines think that unless they die the rivers will
    not move.
They are dying so that the mountain shadows will
    continue to fall east in the afternoon,
So that the beetle can move along the ground near the
    fallen twigs.

9

But if one of those children came near that we have set
    on fire,
Came toward you like a gray barn, walking,
You would howl like a wind tunnel in a hurricane,

You would tear at your shirt with blue hands,
You would drive over your own child's wagon trying
    to back up,
The pupils of your eyes would go wild—

If a child came by burning, you would dance on a
    lawn,
Trying to leap into the air, digging into your cheeks,
You would ram your head against the wall of your
    bedroom
Like a bull penned too long in his moody pen—

If one of those children came toward me with both
    hands
In the air, fire rising along both elbows,
I would suddenly go back to my animal brain,
I would drop on all fours, screaming,
My vocal cords would turn blue; so would yours;
It would be two days before I could play with my
    own children again.

10

I want to sleep awhile in the rays of the sun slanting
    over the snow.
Don't wake me.
Don't tell me how much grief there is in the leaf with
    its natural oils.
Don't tell me how many children have been born
    with stumpy hands
All those years we lived in St. Augustine's shadow.

* * *

Tell me about the dust that falls from the yellow
    daffodil shaken in the restless winds.
Tell me about the particles of Babylonian thought
    that still pass through the earthworm every day.
Don't tell me about "the frightening laborers who do
    not read books."

Now the whole nation starts to whirl,
The end of the Republic breaks off,
Europe comes to take revenge,
The mad beast covered with European hair rushes
    toward the mesa bushes in Mendocino County.
Pigs rush toward the cliff.
The waters underneath part: in one ocean luminous
    globes float up (in them hairy and ecstatic men);
In the other ocean—the Teeth Mother, naked at last.

Let us drive cars
Up
The light beams
To the stars . . .

Then return to earth crouched inside the drop of
    sweat
That falls
From the chin of the Protestant tied in the fire.

V

THE POINT REYES
POEMS

and Related Poems
1 9 6 5 – 8 4

NOVEMBER DAY AT MCCLURE'S BEACH

Alone on the jagged rock at the south end of McClure's Beach. The sky low. The sea grows more and more private, as afternoon goes on; the sky comes down closer; the unobserved water rushes out to the horizon—horses galloping in a mountain valley at night. The waves smash up the rock; I find flags of seaweed high on the worn top, forty feet up, thrown up overnight; separated water still pooled there, like the black ducks that fly desolate, forlorn, and joyful over the seething swells, who never "feel pity for themselves," and "do not lie awake weeping for their sins." In their blood cells the vultures coast with furry necks extended, watching over the desert for signs of life to end. It is not our life we need to weep for. Inside us there is some secret. We are following a narrow ledge around a mountain; we are sailing on skeletal eerie craft over the buoyant ocean.

THE STARFISH

It is low tide. Fog. I have climbed down the cliffs from Pierce Ranch to the tide pools. Now the ecstasy of the low tide, kneeling down, alone. In six inches of clear water I notice a purple starfish—with nineteen arms! It is a delicate purple, the color of old carbon paper, or an attic dress . . . at the webs between the arms sometimes a more intense sunset red glows through. The fingers are relaxed . . . some curled up at the tips . . . with delicate rods . . . apparently globes on top of each, as at World's Fairs, waving about. The starfish slowly moves up the groin of the rock . . . then back down . . . many of its arms rolled up now, lazily, like a puppy on its back. One arm is especially active and curved up over its own body as if a dinosaur were looking behind him.

How slowly and evenly it moves! The starfish is a glacier, going sixty miles a year! It moves over the pink rock, by means I cannot see . . . and into marvelously floating delicate brown weeds. It is about the size of the bottom of a pail. When I reach into it, it tightens and then slowly relaxes. . . . I take an arm and quickly lift. The underside is a pale tan. . . . Gradually, as I watch, thousands of tiny tubes begin rising from all over the underside . . . hundreds in the mouth, hundreds along the nineteen underarms . . . all looking . . . feeling . . . like a man looking for a woman . . . tiny heads blindly feeling for a rock and finding only air.

A purple rim runs along the underside of every arm, with paler tubes. Probably its moving-feet.

I put him back in. He unfolds—I had forgotten how purple he was—and slides down into his rock groin, the snail-like feelers waving as if nothing had happened, and nothing has.

DRIVING WEST IN 1970

My dear children, do you remember the morning
When we climbed into the old Plymouth
And drove west straight toward the Pacific?

We were all the people there were.
We followed Dylan's songs all the way west.
It was Seventy; the war was over, almost;

And we were driving to the sea.
We had closed the farm, tucked in
The flap, and we were eating the honey

Of distance and the word "there."
Oh whee, we're gonna fly
Down into the easy chair. We sang that

Over and over. That's what the early
Seventies were like. We weren't afraid.
And a hole had opened in the world.

We laughed at Las Vegas.
There was enough gaiety
For all of us, and ahead of us was

The ocean. *Tomorrow's*
The day my bride's gonna come.
And the war was over, almost.

WELCOMING A CHILD IN THE
LIMANTOUR DUNES

For Micah

Thinking of a child soon to be born, I hunch down among friendly sand grains. . . . The sand grains love us, for they love whatever lives without force, a young girl who looks out over her life, alone, with no map, no horse, a white dress on. The sand grains love whatever is not rushing blindly forward—I mean the mole who is blinking at the door of his crumbly mole Vatican, and the salmon who one morning senses in her gills the fragrant Oregon waters crashing down. Something seems to love this planet abandoned here at the edge of the Milky Way, and this child floating inside the Pacific of the womb, near the walls, hearing the breakers roaring.

CLIMBING UP MOUNT VISION WITH MY LITTLE BOY

We started up. All the way he held my hand. Sometimes he falls back to bend over a banana slug, then senses how lonely the slug is, and comes running back. He never complained, and we went straight up. How much I love being with him! How much I love to feel his small leafy hand curl around my finger. He holds on, and we are flying through a cloud. On top we hunker down beneath some bushes to get out of the wind, while the girls go off to play, and he tells me the story of the little boy who wouldn't cut off his hair and give it to a witch, and so she changed him into a hollow log! A boy and girl came along, and stepped on the log—and the log said, "Oww!" They put their feet on it again, and the log said, "Oww!" Then they looked inside and saw a boy's jacket sticking out. A little boy was in there! "I can't come out, I've been changed into a hollow log." That's the end, he said.

Then I remembered a bit more—the boy and the girl went to a wise man . . . he corrected me, "It was a wise woman, Daddy," . . . and said, "How can we get him changed back into a little boy?" She said, "Here is a pearl. If a crow asks you for it, give it to him." So they went along. Pretty soon a crow came and said, "Can I have the buttons on your shirt?" The boy said, "Yes." Then the crow said, "Can I have that pearl in your shirt pocket?" "Yes." Then the crow flew up and dropped some moss down the witch's chimney. The chimney got full, the witch started to cough. The crow dropped in some more moss. Then she had to open the door, and run outside! Then the crow took an oyster, a big one, from the Johnson Oyster Company, and flew high into the air, and dropped it right on the witch's head. And that was the end of her. And then the boy was changed back again into a little boy.

The land on top is bare, sweeping, forbidding—so unlike a little boy's mind. I asked him what he liked best about the whole walk. He said it was Bethany (an eight-year-old friend of Mary's) going peepee in her pants while hiding.

CALM MORNING AT DRAKE'S BAY

A sort of roll develops out of the bay, and lays itself all down this long beach. . . . A hiss as the water wall two inches high comes in, steady as lions, or African grass fires. Two gulls with feet the color of a pumpkin walk together on the sand. A snipe settles down . . . then three squawks. . . . The gulls agree to chase it away. Now the wave goes out; the waters mingle so beautifully; it is the mingling after death—the silence, the sweep—so swift!—over darkening sand. The airplane sweeps low over the African field at night, lost, no tin cans burning. The old woman stomps around her house on a cane, no lamp lit yet. . . .

TRESPASSING ON THE PIERCE RANCH

I walk toward Tomales Point over soaked and lonely hills—a wild cat runs away from his inspection of a wet gopher hole as I come near. Wind off the sea. A few sheep, some cows with large udders high above the ocean.

These cliffs are the first land the amazed traveler saw when looking over the rail he suddenly came on a continent . . . in the middle of the endless ocean.

Glancing east, I see the three-quarters moon moving in broad daylight, pale and urgent, through the sky, freeing itself from itself in the clouds. It is a sturdy eye-traveler, sailing eerily forward, orphaned, bold and alone. Formed long ago, it has parted from the Earth as my moon from myself.

Part of me sails steadily through clouds, and the rest of me is down here, among these soaked and lonely hills. These lowlands that are backed by the Coastal Range and again by the Rockies thicken eastward into Nebraska and the plateau that holds up the heavy pueblos, Taos, San Isidro, Isleta.

There the old men hit the boys lightly with twigs as the boys run past, their heels hitting the earth, racing each other to the plaza, where a Douglas fir has been set up with a dead sheep tied to the very top. One of the winter boys arrives first. Then the clowns prepare to unhook the sheep from the sky.

The Dead Seal

I

Walking north toward the point, I come on a dead seal. From a few feet away, he looks like a brown log. The body is on its back, dead only a few hours. I stand and look at him. There's a quiver in the dead flesh: My God, he's still alive. And a shock goes through me, as if a wall of my room had fallen away.

His head is arched back, the small eyes closed; the whiskers sometimes rise and fall. He is dying. This is the oil. Here on its back is the oil that heats our houses so efficiently. Wind blows fine sand back toward the ocean. The flipper near me lies folded over the stomach, looking like an unfinished arm, lightly glazed with sand at the edges. The other flipper lies half underneath. And the seal's skin looks like an old overcoat, scratched here and there—by sharp mussel shells maybe.

I reach out and touch him. Suddenly he rears up, turns over. He gives three cries: Awaark! Awaark! Awaark!—like the cries from Christmas toys. He lunges toward me; I am terrified and leap back, though I know there can be no teeth in that jaw. He starts flopping toward the sea. But he falls over, on his face. He does not want to go back to the sea. He looks up at the sky, and he looks like an old lady who has lost her hair. He puts his chin back down on the sand, rearranges his flippers, and waits for me to go. I go.

2

The next day I go back to say good-bye. He's dead now. But he's not. He's a quarter mile farther up the shore. Today he is thinner, squatting on his stomach, head out. The ribs show more: each vertebra on the back under the coat is visible, shiny. He breathes in and out.

A wave comes in, touches his nose. He turns and looks at me—the eyes slanted; the crown of his head looks like a boy's leather jacket bending over some bicycle bars. He is taking a long time to die. The whiskers white as porcupine quills, the forehead slopes. . . . Good-bye, brother, die in the sound of the waves. Forgive us if we have killed you. Long live your race, your inner tube race, so uncomfortable on land, so comfortable in the ocean. Be comfortable in death then, when the sand will be out of your nostrils, and you can swim in long loops through the pure death, ducking under as assassinations break above you. You don't want to be touched by me. I climb the cliff and go home the other way.

An Octopus

I hear a ticking on the Pacific stones. A white shape is moving in the furry air of the seacoast. The moon narrow, the sea quiet. He comes close; a long time the stick ticks on over the rock faces. Is it a postal employee saddened by the sleet? It comes nearer. I talk. The shape talks, it is a Japanese man carrying a spear and a heavy-bellied little bag. The spear has a hook on the end. What are you looking for, clams? No! Octopus!

Did you get any? I found three. He sits down. I get up and walk over. May I see them? He opens the plastic bag. I turn on the flashlight. Something wet, fantastic, womblike, horse intestine-like. May I take hold of one? His voice smiles. Why not? I reach in. Dry things stick to my hands, like burrs from burdocks, compelling, pleading, dry, poor, in debt. You boil them, then sauté them. I look and cannot find the eyes. He is a cook. He ate them in Japan.

So the octopus is gone now from the mussel-ridden shelf with the low roof, the pool where he waited under the thin moon, but the sea never came back, no one came home, the door never opened. Now he is taken away in the plastic bag, not understood, illiterate.

THE HOCKEY POEM

For Bill Duffy

The Goalie

The Boston College team has gold helmets, under which the long black hair of the Roman centurion curls out. . . . And they begin. How weird the goalies look with their African masks! The goalie is so lonely anyway, guarding a basket with nothing in it, his wide lower legs wide as ducks'. . . . No matter what gift he is given, he always rejects it. . . . He has a number like 1, a name like Mrazek, sometimes wobbling on his legs waiting for the puck, or curling up like a baby in the womb to hold it, staying a second too long on the ice.

The goalie has gone out to mid-ice, and now he sails sadly back to his own box, slowly; he looks prehistoric with his rhinoceros legs; he looks as if he's going to become extinct, and he's just taking his time. . . .

When the players are at the other end, he begins sadly sweeping the ice in front of his house; he is the old witch in the woods, waiting for the children to come home.

2.

The Attack

They all come hurrying back toward us, suddenly, knees dipping like oil wells; they rush toward us wildly,

96

fins waving, they are pike swimming toward us, their gill fins expanding like the breasts of opera singers; no, they are twelve hands practicing penmanship on the same piece of paper. . . . They flee down the court toward us like birds, swirling two and two, hawks hurrying for the mouse, hurrying down wind valleys, swirling back and forth like amoebae on the pale slide, as they sail in the absolute freedom of water and the body, untroubled by the troubled mind, only the body, with wings as if there were no grave, no gravity, only the birds sailing over the cottage far in the deep woods. . . .

Now the goalie is desperate . . . he looks wildly over his left shoulder, rushing toward the other side of his cave, like a mother hawk whose chicks are being taken by two snakes. . . . Suddenly he flops on the ice like a man trying to cover a whole double bed. He has the puck. He stands up, turns to his right, and drops it on the ice at the right moment; he saves it for one of his children, a mother hen picking up a seed and then dropping it. . . .

But the men are all too clumsy, they can't keep track of the puck . . . no, it is the *puck,* the puck is too fast, too fast for human beings, it humiliates them constantly. The players are like country boys at the fair watching the con man—The puck always turns up under the wrong walnut shell. . . .

They come down ice again, one man guiding the puck this time . . . and Ledingham comes down beautifully, like the canoe through white water, or the lover going upstream, every stroke right, like the stallion galloping up the valley surrounded by his mares and colts, how beautiful, like the body and soul crossing in a poem. . . .

3.

The Fight

The player in position pauses, aims, pauses, cracks his stick on the ice, and a cry as the puck goes in! The goalies stands up disgusted, and throws the puck out. . . .

The player with a broken stick hovers near the cage. When the play shifts, he skates over to his locked-in teammates, who look like a nest of bristling owls, owl babies, and they hold out a stick to him. . . .

Then the players crash together, their hockey sticks raised like lobster claws. They fight with slow motions, as if undersea . . . they are fighting over some woman back in the motel, but like lobsters they forget what they're battling for; the clack of the armor plate distracts them, and they feel a pure rage.

Or a fighter sails over to the penalty box, where ten-year-old boys wait to sit with the criminal, who is their hero. . . . They know society is wrong, the wardens are wrong, the judges hate individuality. . . .

4.

The Goalie

And this man with his peaked mask, with slits, how fantastic he is, like a white insect who has given up on evolution in this life; his family hopes to evolve after death, in the grave. He is ominous as a Dark Ages knight . . . the Black Prince. His enemies defeated him in the day, but every one of them died in their beds that night. . . . At his father's funeral, he carried his own head under his arm.

He is the old woman in the shoe, whose house is never clean, no matter what she does. Perhaps this goalie is not a man at all, but a woman, all women; in her cage everything disappears in the end; we all long for it. All these movements on the ice will end, the seats will come down, the stadium walls bare. . . . This goalie with his mask is a woman weeping over the children of men, that are cut down like grass, gulls that stand with cold feet on the ice. . . . And at the end, she is still waiting, brushing away before the leaves, waiting for the new children developed by speed, by war. . . .

TWO SOUNDS WHEN WE SIT BY THE OCEAN

Waves rush up, pause, and drag pebbles back around stones . . . the sound of pebbles going out. . . . It is a complicated sound, as of small sticks breaking, or kitchen sounds heard from another house, the rustling when bodies turn over at night. . . . Now the retreating wave gets to the boulders, drops down over the stones always wet . . . the gentleness of William Carlos Williams after his stroke. . . . Then we hear the sound of harsh death waves that race up the roof of leopard-colored stones, leaving a tiny rattling in the throat as they go out. . . . They leave the ecstatic brown sand stretched out between stones. We know that the anger of some young women is right.

And always another sound: a heavy underground roaring in my ears from the surf farther out, as if the earth were reverberating under the feet of one dancer. That sound is a comforting sound, like the note of Paradise carried to the Egyptian sands; and I hear the driftwood far out singing; the great logs, fifty miles out, still floating in. The water under the waters is singing, what has not yet come to the surface to float, years that are still down somewhere below the chest. Long trunks are out there, too, that have floated all the way from the Pacific islands. . . . And the donkey the disciples will find standing beside the white wall . . .

SITTING ON SOME ROCKS IN SHAW COVE

I sit in a cliff hollow, surrounded by fossils and furry shells. The sea breathes and breathes under the new moon. Suddenly it rises, hurrying into the long crevices in the rock shelves, it rises like a woman's belly as if nine months has passed in a second; rising like the milk to the tiny veins, it overflows like a snake going over a low wall.

I have the sensation that half an inch under my skin there are nomad bands, stringy-legged men with fire-sticks and wide-eyed babies. The rocks with their backs turned to me have something spiritual in them. On these rocks I am not afraid of death; death is like the sound of the motor in an airplane as we fly. And I still haven't found the woman I loved in some former life—how could I, when I have loved only twice on this rock, though twice in the moon, and three times in the rising water. My two daughters run toward me, laughing, arms in the air. A bird with long wings comes flying toward me in the dusk, pumping just over the darkening waves. He has flown around the whole planet; it has taken him centuries. He returns to me the lean-legged runner laughing as he runs through the stringy grasses, and gives back to me my buttons, and the soft sleeves of my sweater.

LOOKING AT A DEAD WREN IN MY HAND

Forgive the hours spent listening to radios, and the words of gratitude I did not say to teachers. I love your tiny ricelike legs, that are bars of music played in an empty church, and the feminine tail, where no worms of Empire have ever slept, and the intense yellow chest that makes tears come. Your tail feathers open like a picket fence, and your bill is brown, with the sorrow of a rabbi whose daughter has married an athlete. The black spot on your head is your own mourning cap.

A HOLLOW TREE

I bend over an old hollow cottonwood stump, still standing, waist-high, and look inside. Early spring. Its Siamese temple walls are all brown and ancient. The halls have been worked on by the intricate ones. Inside the hollow walls there is privacy and secrecy, dim light. And yet some creature has died here.

On the temple floor feathers, gray feathers, many of them with a fluted white tip. Many feathers. In the silence many feathers.

AUGUST RAIN

After a month and a half without rain, at last, in late August, darkness comes at three in the afternoon, a cheerful thunder begins, and then the rain. I set a glass out on a table to measure the rain, and, suddenly buoyant and affectionate, go indoors to find my children. They are upstairs, playing quietly alone in their doll-filled rooms, hanging pictures, thoughtfully moving "the small things that make them happy" from one side of the room to another. I feel triumphant, without need of money, far from the grave.

I walk over the grass, watching the soaked chairs, and the cooled towels, and sit down on my stoop, dragging a chair out with me. The rain deepens. It rolls off the porch roof, making a great puddle near me. The bubbles slide toward the puddle edge, become crowded, and disappear. The black earth turns blacker, it absorbs the rain needles without a sound. The sky is low, everything silent, as when parents are angry. . . . What has failed and been forgiven—the leaves from last year unable to go on, lying near the foundation, dry under the porch, retreat farther into the shadow, they give off a faint hum, as of birds' eggs, or the tail of a dog.

The older we get the more we fail, but the more we fail the more we feel a part of the dead straw of the universe, the corners of barns with cow dung twenty years old, the belt left hanging over the chair back after the bachelor has died in the ambulance on the way to the city. These objects ride us as the child who holds on to the dog's fur; these objects appear in our dreams; they are more and more near us, coming in slowly from the wainscoting; they make our trunks heavy, accumulating between trips; they lie against the ship's side, and will nudge the hole open that lets the water in at last.

WARNING TO THE READER

Sometimes farm granaries become especially beautiful when all the oats or wheat are gone, and wind has swept the rough floor clean. Standing inside, we see around us, coming in through the cracks between shrunken wall boards, bands or strips of sunlight. So in a poem about imprisonment, one sees a little light.

But how many birds have died trapped in these granaries. The bird, seeing the bands of light, flutters up the walls and falls back again and again. The way out is where the rats enter and leave; but the rat's hole is low to the floor. Writers, be careful then by showing the sunlight on the walls not to promise the anxious and panicky blackbirds a way out!

I say to the reader, beware. Readers who love poems of light may sit hunched in the corner with nothing in their gizzard for four days, light failing, the eyes glazed. . . . They may end as a mound of feathers and a skull on the open boardwood floor. . . .

The Mushroom

This white mushroom comes up through the duffy lith on a granite cliff, in a crack that ice has widened. The most delicate light tan, it has the texture of a rubber ball left in the sun too long. To the fingers it feels a little like the tough heel of a foot.

One split has gone deep into it, dividing it into two half-spheres, and through the cut one can peek inside, where the flesh is white and gently naive.

The mushroom has a traveler's face. We know there are men and women in Old People's Homes whose souls prepare now for a trip, which will also be a marriage. There must be travelers all around, supporting us, whom we do not recognize. This granite cliff also travels. Do we know more about our wife's journey or our dearest friends' than the journey of this rock? Can we be sure which traveler will arrive first, or when the wedding will be? Everything is passing away except the day of this wedding.

A Chunk of Amethyst

Held up to the windowlight, the amethyst has elegant corridors that give and take light. The discipline of its many planes suggests that there is no use in trying to live forever. Its exterior is jagged, but in the inner house all is in order. Its corridors become ledges, solidified thoughts that pass each other.

This chunk of amethyst is a cool thing, hard as a dragon's tongue. The sleeping times of the whole human race lie hidden there. When the fingers fold the chunk into the palm, the palm hears organ music, the low notes that make the sins of the whole congregation resonate, and catch the criminal five miles away with a tinge of doubt.

With all its plane, it turns four or five faces toward us at once, and four or five meanings enter the mind. The exhilaration we felt as children returns. . . . We feel the wind on the face as we go downhill, the sled's speed increasing. . . .

VI
LOVING A WOMAN
IN TWO WORLDS

and Related Poems
1973–81

THE THIRD BODY

A man and a woman sit near each other, and they do
    not long
At this moment to be older, or younger, or born
In any other nation, or any other time, or any other
    place.
They are content to be where they are, talking or not
    talking.
Their breaths together feed someone whom we do
    not know.
The man sees the way his fingers move;
He sees her hands close around a book she hands to
    him.
They obey a third body that they share in common.
They have promised to love that body.
Age may come; parting may come; death will come!
A man and a woman sit near each other;
As they breathe they feed someone we do not know,
Someone we know of, whom we have never seen.

The Horses at the Tank

Every breath taken in by the man
Who loves, and the woman who loves,
Goes to fill the water tank
Where the spirit horses drink.

The Whole Moisty Night

The Viking ship sails into the full harbor.
The body meets its wife far out at sea.
Its lamp remains lit the whole moisty night.
Water pours down, faint flute notes in the sound of
    the water.

ONE MORNING

While we were still in our room, we heard reports that hundreds of children had appeared in the village at noon. I said to you, "Ah, a sign." Outside the village walls we met black peacocks and immaculate white ants.

As we climbed the mountainside, tails of long birds brushed our faces. A French band director with a macaw tail waved his baton. You became an oriole nest; I joined you. Summer deepened; long lines of red birds flew south.

By now we had passed the mountain peak, and were going down the other side. We found grains of rice left for us. We both heard a sound; we didn't know what it was. It was all around us. Then we understood it was the sea.

WINTER POEM

The quivering wings of the winter ant
Wait for lean winter to end.
I love you in slow, dimwitted ways,
Hardly speaking, one or two words only.

What caused us each to live hidden?
A wound, the wind, a word, a parent.
Sometimes we wait in a helpless way,
Awkwardly, not whole and not healed.

When we hid the wound, we fell back
From a human to a shelled life.
Now we feel the ant's hard chest,
The carapace, the silent tongue.

This must be the way of the ant,
The winter ant, the way of those
Who are wounded and want to live:
To breathe, to sense another, and to wait.

AT MIDOCEAN

All day I loved you in a fever, holding on to the tail of
    the horse.
I overflowed whenever I reached out to touch you.
My hand moved over your body, covered
With its dress,
Burning, rough, the hand of an animal's foot moving
    over leaves.
The rainstorm retires, clouds open, sunlight
Sliding over ocean water a thousand miles from land.

LISTENING TO THE KÖLN CONCERT

After we had loved each other intently,
We heard notes tumbling together,
In late winter, and we heard ice
Falling from the ends of twigs.

The notes abandon so much as they move.
They are the food not eaten, the comfort
Not taken, the lies not spoken.
The music is my attention to you.

And when the music came again,
Later in the day, I saw tears in your eyes.
I saw you turn your face away
So that others would not see.

When men and women come together,
How much they have to abandon! Wrens
Make their nests of fancy threads
And string ends, animals

Abandon all their money each year.
What is it that men and women leave?
Harder than wrens' doing, they have
To abandon their longing for the perfect.

The inner nest not made by instinct
Will never be quite round,
And each has to enter the nest
Made by the other imperfect bird.

LOVE POEM IN TWOS AND THREES

What kind of people
Are these? Some stammer
Of land, some
Want nothing but light—
No house or land
Thrown away for a woman,
No ample recklessness.
How much I need
A woman's soul, felt
In my own knees,
Shoulders, and hands.
I was born sad!
I am a northern goat
Of winter light,
Up to my knees in snow.
Standing by you, I am
Glad as the clams
At high tide, eerily
Content as the amorous
Ocean owls.

Poem on Sleep

"Then the bright being disguised as a seal dove into
    the deep billows."
I go on loving you after we are asleep.
I know the ledges where we sit all night looking out
    over the briny sea,
And the open places where we coast in sleekness
    through the sea.

And where is the hunter who is cunning? The
    practical part of me?
Oh he is long since gone, dispersed among the bold
    grasses.
The one he does not know of remains afloat and
    awake all night;
He lies on luminous boulders, dives, his coat sleek, his
    eyes open.

The Horse of Desire

"Yesterday I saw a face
That gave off light."
I wrote that the first time
I saw you; now the lines
Written that morning
Are twenty years old.
What is it that
We see and don't see?

When a horse swings
His head, how easily
His shoulders follow.
When the right thing happens,
The whole body knows.
The road covered with stones
Turns to a soft river
Moving among reeds.

I love you in those reeds,
And in the bass
Quickening there.
My love is in the demons
Gobbling the waters,
My desire in their swollen
Foreheads poking
Earthward out of the trees.

The bear between my legs
Has one eye only,
Which he offers
To God to see with.
The two beings below with no
Eyes at all love you
With the slow persistent
Intensity of the blind.

CONVERSATION WITH A HOLY WOMAN
NOT SEEN FOR MANY YEARS

After so many years, I come walking to you.
You say: "You have come after so long?"
I could not come earlier. My shabby mouth,
With its cavernous thirst, ate the seeds of longing
That should have been planted. Awkward and baffled,
Dishonest, I slept. And I dreamt of sand.
Your eyes in sorrow do not laugh.
I say, "I have come after so many years."

TWO MIDDLE-AGED LOVERS

An Etching by Durer

The man and the woman linger under a tree,
Soberly, standing near his horse.
Man and woman hear the low, muttering speech
Instinct makes to instinct.
Their canoe shoots down the narrow channel;
The climber goes rock by rock up the mountainside.
The yaks, hair blowing, disappear into the storm.

IN RAINY SEPTEMBER

In rainy September, when leaves grow down into the
dark,
I put my forehead down to the damp, seaweed-
smelling sand.
The time has come. I have put off choosing for years,
Perhaps whole lives. The fern has no choice but to
live;
For this crime it receives earth, water, and night.

We close the door. "I have no claim on you." Dusk
Comes. You say, "The love I had with you is
enough."
We know we could live apart from one another.
The sheldrake floats apart from the flock.
The oak tree puts out leaves alone on the lonely
hillside.

Men and women before us have accomplished this.
I would see you, and you me, once a year.
We would be two kernels, and not be planted.
We stay in the room, door closed, lights out.
I weep with you without shame and without honor.

THE INDIGO BUNTING

I go to the door often.
Night and summer. Crickets
Lift their cries.
I know you are out.
You are driving
Late through the summer night.

I do not know what will happen.
I have no claim on you.
I am one star
You have as guide; others
Love you, the night
So dark over the Azores.

You have been working outdoors,
Gone all week. I feel you
In this lamp lit
So late. As I reach for it
I feel myself
Driving through the night.

I love a firmness in you
That disdains the trivial
And regains the difficult.
You become part then
Of the firmness of night,
The granite holding up walls.

There were women in Egypt who
Supported with their firmness the stars
As they revolved,
Hardly aware
Of the passage from night
To day and back to night.

I love you where you go
Through the night, not swerving,
Clear as the indigo
Bunting in her flight,
Passing over two
Thousand miles of ocean.

IN THE TIME OF PEONY BLOSSOMING

When I come near the red peony flower
I tremble as water does near thunder,
As the well does when the plates of earth move,
Or the tree when fifty birds leave at once.

The peony says that we have been given a gift,
And it is not the gift of this world.
Behind the leaves of the peony
There is a world still darker, that feeds many.

THE MOOSE

The Arctic moose drinks at the tundra's edge,
Swirling the watercress with his mouth.
How fresh the water is, the coolness of the far North.
A light wind moves through the deep firs.

THE RAM

The ram walks over the minty grass.
The hawk ruffles his shoulder feathers.
Two chooks sit with feathers overlapping.
Just before dark big snowflakes fall.

THE EAGLE

Whenever a man tries to save a woman—
As he once tried to save his mother—
It means that he is married—
To what? To that which
Will tear him to pieces.

Last night while I was sleeping,
I dreamt an eagle had his head
And beak all the way inside
The body of a dead dog.
He raised his head and looked at me.

THE HERON DRINKING

The bird dips to take some water in its bill.
We receive what the nation cannot give.
We are thirsty for the heron
And the lake, the touch of the bill on the water.

In the Month of May

In the month of May, when all leaves open,
I see when I walk how well all things
Lean on each other, how the bees work,
The fish make their living the first day.
Monarchs fly high; then I understand
I love you with what in me is unfinished.

I love you with what in me is still
Changing, what has no head or arms
Or legs, what has not found its body.
And why shouldn't the miraculous,
Caught on this earth, visit
The old man alone in his hut?

And why shouldn't Gabriel, who loves honey,
Be fed with our own radishes and walnuts?
And lovers, tough ones, how many there are
Whose holy bodies are not yet born.
Along the roads, I see so many places
I would like us to spend the night.

A Dream of an Afternoon with a Woman I Did Not Know

I woke up and went out. Not yet dawn.
A rooster claimed he was the sickle moon.
The windmill was a ladder that ended at a gray cloud.
A feed grinder was growling at a nearby farm.

Frost has made clouds of the weeds overnight.
In my dream, we stopped for coffee. We sat alone
Near a fireplace, near delicate cups.
I loved that afternoon, and the rest of my life.

Love Poem About a Spinning Wheel

I think we were tinkers once or Gypsies wandering
    around Hardanger,
Listening to the chandeliers ringing together
On the windy afternoon of some stubborn century.

The Norwegian manor house or castle stood on a
    hill—
It was really a farm—and each dawn animal
Noses left some of their warmth near the hand-hewn
    boards.

Husbands and wives, beneath lintels painted blue and
    orange,
Climbed into their cramped and boxy beds.
Stiff at first, they relaxed and rolled down the incline
    of sleep.

The twelve-stringed fiddler awoke about midnight,
    looking contained, and reported
That angels had begun visiting old men.
The harness-maker and his wife reported that fierce
    people with tails were approaching.

While the help were making römmegröt, a monster
    sitting
On the kitchen floor asked for fruit,
Then wept for his sins. Later he helped to repair the
    spinning wheel.

Within a year, the spinning wheel had children, and
    still later joined
A pilgrimage to St. James
Of Compostela, walking on two furry legs no one had
    noticed.

THE STORM

A sadness comes when we think back.
The car says, "I will bring you somewhere."
Confusion says, "Is it all clear?"
The sadness says, "A storm is coming."

We were still warming up the car
When the storm came. Like all storms,
It lacked subtlety and obeyed
Something or someone irresistible.

Nine people stood looking out at the car.
There wasn't room for everyone.
Someone would be left behind
In the cold house. Human longing

Says, "I know there's a better place."
The car says, "Let's stop talking."
Confusion says that we're quite clear about it.
And the storm says, "Here I come."

A Man and a Woman and a Blackbird

A man and a woman
are one.
A man and a woman and a blackbird
are one.

—*Wallace Stevens*

When the two rivers
Join in the cloudy chamber,
So many alien nights
In our twenties, alone
On interior mountains,
Forgotten. Blackbirds
Walk around our feet
As if they shared
In what we know.
We know and we don't know
What the heron feels
With his wing-
Tip feathers stretched
Out in the air above
The flooded lake,
Or the truffled constellations
The pig sees
Past his wild snout.
A man and a woman
Sit near each other. On
The windowpane
Ice.

The man says: "How
Is it
I have never loved
Ice before?
If I have not loved ice,
What have I loved?
Loved the dead
In their Sumerian
Fish-cloaks?
The vultures celebrating?
The soldiers
And the poor?"
And yet
For one or two
Moments,
In our shared grief
And exile,
We hang our harps
On the willows,
And the willows
Join us,
And the man
And the woman
And the blackbird are one.

THE ANT ON THE BOARD

It is not only the ant that walks on the carpenter's
    board alone,
Nor the March turtle on his boulder surrounded by
    March water . . .
I know there are whitecaps that are born and die
    alone.
There is a rocky pasture, and a new one nearby, with a
    path between.

I know there are branchy stalks, dropped to the
    ground last summer,
And tires, half worn-down, lifted to the gas station
    owner's rack.
All of them I saw today, and all of them were dear to
    me,
And the rough-barked young cottonwood alone on
    the windy shore.

What we experience is not the ant on the carpenter's
    board
Only, nor the March turtle on his wet boulder,
Nor the rising whirlwind, nor the certainty, nor the
    steady gaze,
Nor the meeting by the altar, nor the rising sun only.

A Love That I Have in Secret

Who is this in me who loves you so?
It must be four fiery men;
They make up a man who loves you.
His grief and his music cannot
Be explained: it is wound inside
An ocean shell, held up to the ears
Of old Egyptian ladies soon to be born.

Do these speculations confuse adultery
With light and make it sound civilized?
Say then that it is a Northern love,
A barbarous and shadowy thing,
A turbid river where the moose drinks,
His antlers lifted as my body above you
When we make love upon the waters.

THE RED SEA

November snowfall settles on the rented house;
It makes the shore, the rocks, and the forest floor
    white.
But cedar trunks, with their shallow roots,
Whether erect or prone, look black in this light.
Snow falls into the lake minute after minute.
What is smaller dissolves into what is greater.
Should we be afraid? All kernels with beards,
All wheat grains with hulls, the hooves
Of the red donkey beat into the dust.
Old storybooks warn us about this fall.
The Red Sea drowns those who do not believe.

COME LIVE WITH ME

Driving among the moraine hills
Near Battle Lake, around Vining.
I admire the hand-cut fenceposts,
The orchards, the hay stored for winter.

I want you to come with me and see
The cowtracks winding down the hills,
The chunks of oak piled for winter,
The small lakes folded in and gleaming.

An Evening When the Full Moon
Rose as the Sun Set

The sun goes down in the dusty April night.
"You know it could be alive!"
The sun is round, massive, compelling, sober, on fire.
It moves swiftly through the tree-stalks of the Lundin
    grove as we drive past. . . .
The legs of a bronze god walking at the edge of the
    world, unseen by many,
On his archaic errands, doubled up on his own
    energy.
He guides his life by his dreams,
When we look again he is gone.

Turning toward Milan, we see the other one, the
    moon, whole and rising.
Three wild geese make dark spots in that part of the
    sky.
Under the shining one the pastures leap forward,
Grass fields rolling as in October, the sow-colored
    fields near the river.
The rising one lights the pair of pintails alert in the
    shallow pond.
It shines on those faithful to each other, alert in the
    early night,
And the life of faithfulness goes by like a river,
With no one noticing it.

VII
THIS BODY IS MADE
OF CAMPHOR AND
GOPHERWOOD
1973–80

WALKING SWIFTLY

When I wake, I hear sheep eating apple peels just outside the screen. The trees are heavy, soaked, cold, and hushed, the sun just rising. All seems calm, and yet somewhere inside I am not calm. We live in wooden buildings made of two-by-fours, making the landscape nervous for a hundred miles. And the emperor, when he was sixty, called for rhinoceros horn, for sky-blue phoenix eggs shaped from veined rock, dipped in rooster blood. Around him the wasps keep guard, the hens continue their patrol, the oysters open and close all questions. The heat inside the human body grows, it does not know where to throw itself—for a while it knots into will, heavy, burning, sweet, then into generosity, that longs to take on the burdens of others, and then into mad love. The artist walks swiftly to his studio and carves oceanic waves into the dragon's mane.

BLESSINGS ON THE BODY'S INNER FURNACE

Perhaps we should thank the stomach first, who has learned how to magically father the children of heat. How delicately the body carries into its house the loaves of carrot, onion, and brown rice, and throws these heat-seeds into the furnace, near where the furnace-keeper lies sleeping, all awash in awakening murders.

And the liver, the ilium, the duodenum, the jejunum, the caecum, the foregut and the hindgut gather, secrete, comfort, and hatch the new food. We are companions to the bark-eating porcupines out for their morning walk, and bosom friends of the mineral stars, whose inner furnaces heated them so well they produce their coppery light. And the thyroid and the pancreas call up the heat preserved for eras under the ice, bits of sunlight that got caught in a stone, tiny sexual flames in the sparrow's foot, the fire from the dry shavings in our tongue. Because of that we can exchange sparks of light with another's eyes when we meet our lover on the dance floor at someone else's wedding.

Our brains then go about warmed and fiery, and with one note they can explode into the cello concertos and can imagine the giant blinking at the top of the bean stalk . . . his barbarous fingers scratching his head.

Blessings then on the stomach, and all cookstoves, all kilns, and cauldrons, all urns, and tinderboxes, all retorts, alchemical ovens, and corncob ranges.

Wings Folding Up

The cucumbers are thirsty, their big leaves turn away from the wind. I water them after supper; the hose lies curled near the rhubarb. The wind sound blows through the head; a smile appears on the sitter's face as he sits down under a tree. Words comfort us, the sunken islands speak to us. . . .

Is this world animal or vegetable? Others love us, the cabbages love the earth, the earth is fond of the heavens—a new age comes close through the dark, an elephant's trunk waves in the darkness, so much is passing away, so many disciplines already gone; but the energy in the double flower does not falter; the wings fold up around the sitting man's face. And these cucumber leaves are my body, and my thighs, and toes stretched out in the wind. . . . Well, waterer, how will you get through this night without water?

Going Out to Check the Ewes

My friend, this body is food for the thousand dragons of the air, each dragon light as a needle. This body loves us, and carries us home from our hoeing.

It is ancient, and full of the bales of sleep. In its vibrations the sun rolls along under the earth; the spouts over the ocean curl into our stomach. Water revolves, making spouts seen by skull eyes at midocean. This body of herbs and gopherwood, this blessing, is a lone ridge patrolled by water. . . . I get up, morning is here. The stars are still out; the black winter sky looms over the unborn lambs. The barn is cold before dawn, the gates slow.

This body longs for itself far out at sea, it floats in the black heavens, it is a brilliant being, locked in the prison of human dullness. . . .

FOUR ADVENTURES OF THE SOUL

Let's imagine that our soul is made up of twenty horses and their riders. They come out of the East somewhere, capable riders, capable horses. Trials are coming! But the riders seem experienced. They must have run this course before.

When the riders are still inside the womb, they meet the cliff of the mother. Below them is a river, and death comes behind. But the cliff is too dangerous! Some stay, and die in the womb. A voice says, "Jump." This is a hard trial: The heart beats just thinking of it. So when we see a baby just born, we are seeing a wet horse and a wet rider.

Now the remaining riders meet in the forest of greed. Your task is to rob the neighboring rider. No one can see you in those immense trees, and there is shadow. If you hesitate, you die. Some riders are driven into trees, others killed, fleeing, by low-lying branches—never so generous or trusting again. The rider comes out with eyes black with soot flakes, darkened forever, from now on watching the angels with amazement, like doomed Cain gazing into Paradise.

The next test is looking. The horses stop; both horse and rider look into the still water. Everywhere in the trees there are mirrors. Some riders ascend into the sky; others disappear into the black on the backs of the mirrors. Many are lost. The riders who survive carry on their features for the rest of their lives the sorrow of Rembrandt's face.

Now they meet their fourth trial—flesh. It is a Garden. Elephant trunks reach lazily up into tree branches; gazelles hurry over the plain, legs flashing, flock on flock, even the monkeys have hair. Horses gallop through miles of creatures. They slow and become confused among so many gentle animals. The riders look to the side and behind them, turning in their saddles to see the large animals peacefully grazing behind.

WE LOVE THIS BODY

My friend, this body is made of energy compacted and whirling. It is the wind that carries the henhouse down the road dancing, and an instant later lifts all four walls apart. It is the horny thumbnail of the retired railway baron, over which his children skate on Sunday; it is the forehead bone that does not rot, and the woman priest's hair still fresh among Shang ritual things. . . .

We love this body as we love the day we first met the person who led us away from this world, as we love the gift we gave one morning on impulse, in a fraction of a second, that we still see every day, as we love the human face, fresh after lovemaking, more full of joy than a wagonload of hay.

FINDING THE FATHER

This body offers to carry us for nothing—as the ocean carries logs—so on some days the body wails with its great energy, it smashes up the boulders, lifting small crabs, that flow around the sides. Someone knocks on the door: we do not have time to dress. He wants us to come with him through the blowing and rainy streets, to the dark house. We will go there, the body says, and there find the father whom we have never met, who wandered out in a snowstorm the night we were born, who then lost his memory, and has lived since longing for his child, whom he saw only once . . . while he worked as a shoemaker, as a cattle herder in Australia, as a restaurant cook who painted at night. When you light the lamp you will see him. He sits there behind the door . . . the eyebrows so heavy, the forehead so light . . . lonely in his whole body, waiting for you.

THE CRY GOING OUT OVER PASTURES

I love you so much with this curiously alive and lonely body. My body is a young hawk sitting on a tree by the Mississippi, in early spring, before any green has appeared on the earth beneath. Some days walnut hollows in my chest fill with crackling light and shadows. There birds drink from water drops. . . . My body loves you with what it extracts from the prudent man, hunched over his colony of lizards; and with that it loves you madly, beyond all rules and conventions. Even the six holes in the flute move about under the dark man's fingers, and the piercing cry goes out over the grown-up pastures no one visits at dusk except the deer, out of all enclosures, who has never seen any bed but his own of wild grass.

I first met you when I had been alone for nine days, and now my lonely hawk body longs to be with you, whom it remembers . . . it knew how close we are, we would always be. There is death but also this closeness, this joy when the bee rises into the air above his hive to find the sun, to become the son, and the traveler moves through exile and loss, through murkiness and failure, to touch the earth again of his own kingdom and kiss the ground. . . .

What shall I say of this? I say, praise to the first man who wrote down this joy clearly, for we cannot remain in love with what we cannot name. . . .

THE OWLETS AT NIGHTFALL

The sun is sinking. Each minute the air darker. The night thickens near the ground, pulls my body down to it. And if my body is earth, then what? Then I am down here, thickening as night comes on. The moon will float up there. Some part of me is up there too. How far it is up to that part!

There are earth things, earthly, joined, they are snuggled down in one manger, one sweep of arms holds them, one clump of pine, the owlets sit together in one hollow tree. . . .

When night comes what has been sun in me all day will drop underneath the earth, and travel sizzling along the underneath-ocean-darkness path. . . . There a hundred developed saints lie stretched out, throwing bits of darkness onto the road.

At midnight what has been moon in me will also vanish. I will go down toward utter darkness and find myself in Joseph's prison cell telling dreams to the baker.

The Lover's Body As a Community of Protozoa

This body is made of bone and excited protozoa . . . and it is with my body that I love the fields. How do I know what I feel but what the body tells me? Erasmus thinking in the snow, translators of Virgil who burn up the whole room, the man in furs reading the Arabic astrologer falls off his three-legged stool in astonishment—this is the body, so beautifully carved inside, with the curves of the inner ear, and the husk so rough, knuckle-brown.

As we walk we enter the magnetic fields of other bodies, and every smell we take in the communities of protozoa see; and a being inside leaps up toward it, as a horse rears at the starting gate. When you and I come near each other, we are drawn down into the sweetest pools of slowly circling energies, slowly circling smells.

Each seed throws itself down before the dawn,
And the night opens itself out behind it,
And inside its own center it lives!

So the space between two people diminishes; it grows less and less; no one to weep; they merge at last. The sound that pours from the fingertips awakens clouds of cells far inside the other's body, and beings unknown to us start out on a pilgrimage to their Savior, to their holy place. Their holy place is a small black stone that they remember from Protozoic times, when it was rolled away from a door.

The clouds of cells awaken, intensify, swarm; and they dance inside a ray of sunlight so thin we cannot even see it. To the cells, each ray is a vast palace with thousands of rooms. From the cells, praise sentences begin to rise to the man and woman singing in the room. A voice says: "Now do you still remain ungrateful? Do you still say there is no road?"

For Lewis Thomas
and his The Lives of the Cell

We walk together through the new snow. No one has walked through it or looked at it. The deep snow makes the sound the porgies hear near the ocean floor, the hum the racer hears the moment before his death, the sound that lifts the buoyant swimmer in the channel.

Four pigeon grass stalks, scarce and fine, lift their heads above the snow. They are four heron legs moving in white morning fog, the musical thoughts that rise as the pianist sits down at her table, the body laboring before dawn to understand its dream.

In our dream, we walk along a stone wall, and pause at an open gate. We look in at an orchard, where a fount of water is rising in the air. We see armed men lying asleep all around the fountain, each with his sword lying under him.

And the orchard keeper . . . where is he?

BLESSINGS ON THE DWELLER

There is a dweller in the dark cabin.
Who is this, someone hearing and telling?
The relative has come, the dark ocean shell.
There is something solid, a dweller in the dark cabin.

The face of the cabin awakens—
What the savage loves in his madness.
The cavern itself wakes up. There is a traveler—
He has to be awake—sleeping in the cabin.

Far down in my dream, I dreamt a bearded fish,
An old one, immense, slipped into my arms.
The traveler gone so long has returned.
There is a dweller in the dark cabin.

The linen merchants find Joseph singing.
Small grains of thread join into longer strings,
Indistinguishable from music when they join,
Something mingling, continual, eternal.

Who is that? A man travels here and there,
Something slowly gains solidity in November air.
Our relative from the lair and the shell has come.
There is a dweller in the dark cabin.

VIII
THE MAN IN THE
BLACK COAT TURNS
1980–84

Snowbanks North of the House

Those great sweeps of snow that stop suddenly six
    feet from the house . . .
Thoughts that go so far.
The boy gets out of high school and reads no more
    books;
The son stops calling home.
The mother puts down her rolling pin and makes no
    more bread.
And the wife looks at her husband one night at a
    party, and loves him no more.
The energy leaves the wine, and the minister falls
    leaving the church.
It will not come closer—
The one inside moves back, and the hands touch
    nothing, and are safe.

The father grieves for his son, and will not leave the
    room where the coffin stands.
He turns away from his wife, and she sleeps alone.

And the sea lifts and falls all night, the moon goes on
    through the unattached heavens alone.
The toe of the shoe pivots
In the dust . . .
And the man in the black coat turns, and goes back
    down the hill.
No one knows why he came, or why he turned away,
    and did not climb the hill.

THE SENSE OF DECLINE

The Farallones seals clubbed,
Whales gone, tortoises
Taken from islands
To fill the holds; the Empire

Dying in its provincial cities.
No one to repair the baths;
Farms turned over
To soldiers; the judges corrupt.

The wagon behind bounces,
Breaking on boulders, back
And forth, slowly smashed
To pieces. This crumbling

Darkness is a reality
Too, the feather
On the snow, the rooster's
Half-eaten body nearby.

And other worlds I do not see:
The Old People's Home
At dusk, the slow
Murmur of conversation.

NIGHT FROGS

I wake and find myself in the woods, far from the
    castle.
The train hurtles through lonely Louisiana at night.
The sleeper turns to the wall; delicate
Aircraft dive toward earth.

A woman whispers to me, urges me to speak truths.
"I am afraid you won't be honest with me."
More than half of the moon rolls on in shadow.
Loons wheel cries through lower waters.

Some invisible being with hooves tramples
The grasses while the horses are asleep.
Something flat slips under the door
And lies exhausted on the floor in the morning.

I threw some parts of me away at ten,
Others at twenty, a lot around twenty-eight.
I wanted to thin myself out as a wire is thinned.
Is there enough left of me now to be honest?

The lizard moves stiffly over November roads.
How much I am drawn toward my parents! I walk
    back
And forth, looking toward the old landing.
Night frogs give out the croak of the planet turning.

My Wife's Painting

1

I walk on a gravel path through cut-over
Woods. November's bare light has arrived.
I come at dusk
Where, sheltered by poplars, a low pond lies.
The sun abandons the sky, speaking through cold
    leaves.

2

This Tang painting is called *The Six Philosophers.*
Five Chinamen talk in the open-walled house,
Exchanging poems.
Only one is outdoors, looking over
The cliff, being approached from below by rolling
    mists.

3

A deer comes down the bare slope toward me,
Sees me, turns away, back up the hill
Into the lone trees.
It is a doe out in the cold and air alone.
It is the woman turned away from the philosopher's
    house.

4

It's an old, long story. After Heraclitus dies,
The males sink down to a-pathy,
To not-suffering.
When you shout at them, they don't reply.
They turn their face toward the crib wall, and die.

5

My wife showed me yesterday her new
Painting. One bird of hers, a lively one,
Had come.
It was a large bird with big feet,
And stubby wings, arrows lightly stuck in the arms.

VISITING EMILY DICKINSON'S GRAVE
WITH ROBERT FRANCIS

Robert Francis has moved, since his stroke, into town, and he takes me to the cemetery. A black iron fence closes the graves in, its ovals delicate as wine stems. They resemble those chapel windows on the main Aran island, made narrow in the fourth century so that not too much rain would drive in. . . . It is April, clear and dry. Curls of grass rise around the nearby gravestones.

The Dickinson house is not far off. She arrived here one day, at fifty-six, Robert says, carried over the lots between by six Irish laboring men, when her brother refused to trust her body to a carriage. The coffin was darkened with violets and pine boughs, as she covered the immense distance between the solid Dickinson house and this plot . . .

The distance *is* immense, the distances through which Satan and his helpers rose and fell, oh vast areas, the distances between stars, between the first time love is felt in the sleeves of the dress, and the death of the person who was in that room. . . . the distance between the feet and head as you lie down, the distance between the mother and father, through which we pass reluctantly.

Exultation is the going
Of the inland soul to sea,
Past the houses, past the headlands
Into deep Eternity.

Emily is sarcastic: "My family addresses an Eclipse every morning, which they call their 'Father.'"

As we leave the cemetery, Robert says, "The apartment is small, but I took it because I could see her grave from my window." He has given his life to seeing what is far away. He used to serve a visitor—in a small glass—wine made from his own dandelions. "Can you mistake us? . . . For this I have abandoned all my other lives."

MOURNING PABLO NERUDA

Water is practical,
Especially in
August.
Faucet water
That drops
Into the buckets
I carry
To the young
Willow trees
Whose leaves have been eaten
Off by grasshoppers.
Or this jar of water
That lies next to me
On the car seat
As I drive to my shack.
When I look down,
The seat all
Around the jar
Is dark,
For water doesn't intend
To give, it gives
Anyway,
And the jar of water
Lies
There quivering
As I drive
Through a countryside

Of granite quarries,
Stones
Soon to be shaped
Into blocks for the dead,
The only
Thing they have
Left that is theirs.

For the dead remain inside
Us, as water
Remains
Inside granite—
Hardly at all—
For their job is to
Go
Away,
And not come back,
Even when we ask them,
But water
Comes to us—
It doesn't care
About us, it goes
Around us, on the way
To the Minnesota River,
To the Mississippi River,
To the Gulf,
Always closer
To where
It has to be.

No one lays flowers
On the grave
Of water,
For it is not
Here,
It is
Gone.

FIFTY MEN SITTING TOGETHER

1

After a long walk in the woods clear-cut for lumber,
Lit up by only a few young pines,
I turn home,
Drawn to water. A band of shadow
Softens half the lake,
Draws the shadow
Down from westward hills.
It is a massive
Masculine shadow—
Fifty men sitting together
In hall or crowded room,
Lifting something indistinct
Up into the resonating night.

2

Near shore, reeds stand about in groups
Unevenly as if they might
Finally ascend
To the sky all together!
Each reed has its own
Thin thread
Of darkness inside so
It is relaxed
And rooted in the mud
And snail shells under the sand.
So the son who has lived

Protected by the mother lives protected
By reeds in the joy of the half darkness.

3

The woman stays in the kitchen, and does not want
To waste fuel by lighting a lamp,
As she waits
For the drunk husband to come home.
Then she serves him
Food in silence.
What does the son do?
He loses courage,
Cleaves to her,
Goes outdoors to feed with wild
Things, pulls away
From brother and father, stays
Safe, in the reeds, admires the sky, ascends.

4

How far he is from working men when he is forty!
From all men! The men singing
Chant far out
On the water grounded in downward shadow.
He cannot go there
Because he
Wants and needs to climb.
He is not ready

Yet to grieve.
The dark comes down slowly,
The way snow falls,
Or herds pass a cave mouth
I look up at the other shore; it is night.

THE VISIT TO HAWAII

This morning I have gone alone
To write by the ocean,
And watch the fish
Between rocks.
The ocean approaches
And recedes, rolling in
On its black lava base.
Some power I cannot see
Moves these small fish.
So many things happen
When no one is watching,
Perhaps *because*
No one is watching.
Pirates bring their ship in
When night is full;
The dancer grows beautiful
After men see her
No longer; Marlene's
Movie becomes clear
When all the actors
Are dead. Earth
Is a thicket of thistles
Waiting for the Wild Man.
Everything is in motion,
Even what is still.
The planet turns, and cows
Wait for the grassblades
To come rushing to their mouths.

Yesterday Peter and I
Arrived on the island
To visit Iolani Lauhine,
The sacred dancer.
After we located her
Temple and found it closed,
We took a motel room
Nearby and slept.
About four I heard,
Waking, the sound
Of shoe soles
Scuffling the rug.
I looked over;
Peter was asleep,
Silent, motionless
In his bed. When
I spoke his name,
The sound stopped.

3

At breakfast I waited.
Peter said:
"I dreamt last night
I opened the balcony
Door and flew
Toward Iolani's
Temple, saw it ahead,
But then grew tired
And turned back. Marie—

Whom you met
In Honolulu—stood
Below in the courtyard,
Looking up kindly
At me. I saw you
At the balcony door
As if urging me in.
Once inside
You were gone.
Sarah, or some
Woman like her,
Stood, changed,
Inside the room
In the mood to kill,
With claw feet and hands.
 I didn't know what to
Do—to fight or to flee.
I could hear my
Tennis shoes rubbing
On the carpet
When I couldn't decide."

4

Peter and I must
Have some defect
Of sight in common,
Or I would not
Have heard the shoes.
"I am afraid that you
Won't be honest with me."

"I was once with
Another man's wife;
The husband came looking
For me dropping shot-
gun shells in the corridor."

And Peter, months
Later, took a stone home
From an old holy site.
The next time he dove
Into the Pacific,
He broke his neck.
From the hospital room
He had the stone
Brought back to its place.

How many stones have
I stolen from Her?
It is a raw way I have
Around time and the pearl.
Not different from taking
Logs away from the mountains.
Pearls turn to bones.
"You will need four
Golden altars," the Gypsy
Woman said
To me, "to remove
The curse . . . "

THE WINEMAKER AND THE CAPTAIN

1

When a man like me steps out at dawn, it seems to him that he has lived his whole life to create something dark. All our work is inside the wine barrels in the hold of the ship. The casks roll about when the ship rolls, and no one on board knows what is in the casks but the captain.

2

The captain stands looking out over the taffrail in the dark, drawn by what follows in shoals behind him. Behind him, fins sail with intense forward strokes. The ship is going to a harbor the captain has chosen, and the casks are rolling. That is all we know.

3

His ship remained tied to the dock for months as the captain lay ill on his pallet in the seaman's home, imagining the covers were a Medusa with his mother's face. And one day as he woke he was already on board. It must be that he hired the seamen, and bought the supplies, while still asleep. Now the ship is moving, and what does he know about those men he has hired? What are the islands like, where they were born; whom do they kneel to at night, fanning a fire of pencil shavings? Or was the seaman born in a farmhouse in Montana? Did he then pass into prison, and through it, as the earthworm passes through thoughtless soil?

4

Now the wine and the ship are passing over the Equator, for the wine's seasoning. And the winemaker, what of him? How many men and women, before we were born, have labored to produce the vines? First the grapes had to be brought from Europe and a climate found, calm and protective; then ground scouted out, difficult to discover with the unknown acids and mineral traces. And it takes so long for the vines to mature. Finally when they are grown, they are tough, twisted, resembling intense dwarf houses. And the winemaker still has to wait so many years before he can bring four casks to the ship.

5

The captain is still alone on the ship, alone among the ocean-flying terns, the great hooded mergansers flopping at early dusk light over the sparse waves they have never been introduced to. . . . Mist suddenly appears at midocean. . . . No assurances in the ocean.

6

When someone says, "You are a good captain!" you have only to reply, "I am not the captain!" When another says, "You make good wine," you have to reply, "I am not the winemaker." Who am I? So when a man like me steps out of the house at dawn, and breathes in the air, it seems to him that he has lived his whole life to create something dark!

THE PRODIGAL SON

The Prodigal Son is kneeling in the husks.
My friend, the steering column in his chest,
Cried: "Don't let me die, Doctor!"
The swine go on feeding in the sunlight.

When he folds his hands, his knees
On corncobs, he sees the smoke of ships
Floating off the isles of Tyre and Sidon,
And father beyond father beyond father.

An old man once, being dragged across
The floor by his shouting son, cried:
"Don't drag me any farther than that crack on the
        floor—
I only dragged my father that far!"

So this dragging of father and son goes on
Century after century after century.
There are brothers, some favorites, some
Not. Neither brother gets what he wants.

My father is seventy-five years old.
Looking at his face, I look into water.
How difficult it is! Under the water
There's a door that the pigs have gone through.

ELEVEN O'CLOCK AT NIGHT

I lie alone in my bed; cooking and stories are over at last, and some peace comes. And what did I do today? I wrote down some thoughts on sacrifice that other people had, but couldn't relate them to my own life. I brought my daughter to the bus—on the way to Minneapolis for a haircut—and I waited twenty minutes with her in the somnolent hotel lobby. I wanted the mail to bring some praise for my ego to eat, and was disappointed. I added up my bank balance, and found only $65, when I need over a thousand to pay the bills for this month alone. So this is how my life is passing before the grave?

The walnut of my brain glows. I feel it irradiate the skull. I am aware of the consciousness I have, and I mourn the consciousness I do not have.

Stubborn things lie and stand around me—the walls, a bookcase with its few books, the footboard of the bed, my shoes that lie against the blanket tentatively, as if they were animals sitting at table, my stomach with its curved demand. I see the bedside lamp, and the thumb of my right hand, the pen my fingers hold so trustingly. There is no way to escape from these. Many times in poems I have escaped—from myself. I sit for hours and at last see a pinhole in the top of the pumpkin, and I slip out that pinhole, gone! The genie expands and is gone; no one can get him back in the bottle again; he is hovering over a car cemetery somewhere.

Now more and more I long for what I cannot escape from. The sun shines on the side of the house across the street. Eternity is near, but it is not *here*. My shoes, my thumbs, my stomach, remain inside the room, and for that there is no solution. Consciousness comes so slowly, half our life passes, we eat and talk asleep—and for that there is no solution. Since Pythagoras died the world has gone down a certain path, and I cannot change that. Someone not in my family invented the microscope, and Western eyes grew the intense will to pierce down through its darkening tunnel. Air itself is willing without pay to lift the 707's wing, and for that there is no solution. Pistons and rings have appeared in the world; valves usher gas vapor in and out of the theater box ten times a second; and for that there is no solution. Something besides my will loves the woman I love. I love my children, though I did not know them before they came. I change every day. For the winter dark of late December there is no solution.

Kennedy's Inauguration

Sister de Chantal hands
Me the sticky pod
Of the sweet gum tree.
New to me, its the size
Of a cow's eyeball, brown
And prickly. Its seeing
Is all gone, finished,
Exploded out
Through the eyeholes.
I turn it in my palm,
It pricks the tender skin.

The hard-edged eye-
Holes resemble hen
Beaks widening in fear.
Are the dogs coming?
Where an ear
Should be, another
Beak is opening, where
A comb should be, another
Beak is opening. Fear
Of the dogs makes
The cries more hoarse.

And what did I do today?
I drove the long way twice
So as not to pass
The funeral home.

I had three conversations,
All distant. If I know
So well how to live,
Then why am I frightened?
A man's head has been
Broken by a cannonball,
One eye dangles out.

King Leopold's men
Set up rubber plantations,
Bring Bantus in
To bleed the trees. Some
Skip work. "If he's
A father, the best thing
Is to cut off the hands."
A photographer catches
The scene: The son's hands
Lie on the ground
Between the father's feet.

Nineteen Thirty-eight:
The Brown Shirts arrive,
Take women away
Into breeding hotels,
Jews and Gypsies
Bleed the trees.
It's all prepared.
Marilyn Monroe is there;
I see her drugged
Arm hanging out

Over the side of the bed.
Out of her back comes the Marine's
Cry for the medic.
His foot is lying a few
Feet away. His
Lips are open, the brain
Is missing—only
The throat and the cry are there.
And the President
In the cold, the back of his head
Still intact, lays
One hand on the Bible.

An Anecdote About My Father

Fresh waters wash past the tidal sands
Into the delta, wash past clear
Bars and are gone.
When water mingles
Into water, who knows when it "dies"?

The doctor said: "No more children, that's it."
But Bertha and Henry wanted this child.
The doctor stands
By the bed, but Bertha
Dies, her breath ends, her knees quiver and are still.

Her husband will not lie quiet.
He throws himself against the wall.
Men come to hold him down.
My father is there,
Sits by the bed long night after night.

KNEELING DOWN TO LOOK INTO A CULVERT

I kneel down to peer into a culvert.
The other end seems far away.
One cone of light floats in the shadowed water.
That's how our children will look when we are dead.

I kneel near the floating shadowy water.
On my knees, I am half inside the tunnel—
Blue sky widens the far end—
Darkened by the shadowy insides of the steel.

Are my children all born? I walk on further.
I pass a pond of rainwater on the field.
I have seen this lake before. . . . it is a lake
I return to each time my children are grown.

I have fathered so many children and returned
To this lake with its grayish, flat, slate banks,
Low arctic bushes. A water serpent lives
There, throwing water drops off his head.

For a thousand years, I stay there alone, with no
Duties, living as I live! In order to be reborn,
I fight. A feathery head pokes from the water.
I fight—it's time—it's right—and am torn to pieces
    fighting.

WORDS RISING

I open my journal, write a few
Words with green ink, and suddenly
Fierceness enters me, stars
Begin to revolve, and pick up
Alligator dust from under the ocean.
Writing vowels, I feel the bushy
Tail of the Great Bear
Reach down and brush the seafloor.

All those deaths we lived in the sunlit
Shelves of the Dordogne, the thousand
Tunes we sang to the skeletons
Of Papua, and all those times
We died—wounded—under the cloak
Of an animal's sniffing, all these moments
Return, and the grassy nights when
We ran in the moonlight for hours.

Watery syllables come welling
Up. When a man or woman
Feeds a few words with private grief,
The shame we knew before we could
Invent the wheel, then words grow.
The old earth-fragrance remains
In the word "and." We experience
"The" in its lonely suffering.

We are bees then; our honey is language.
Now the honey lies stored in caves
Beneath us, and the sound of words
Carries what we have forgotten.
We see a million hands with dusty
Palms turned up inside each
Verb. And there are eternal vows
Held inside the word "Jericho."

Blessings then on the man who labors
In his room writing stanzas on the lamb.
And blessings on the woman who picks the brown
Seeds of solitude in afternoon light
Out of the black seeds of loneliness.
Blessings on the dictionary maker, huddled
Among his bearded words and on the setter of songs
Who sleeps at night inside his violin case.

For Richard Eberhart

IX

MEDITATIONS ON
THE INSATIABLE
SOUL
1990–94

Time Runs Backward After Death

1

Samson, grinding bread for widows and orphans,
Forgets he is wronged, and the answers
The Philistines wrangled out of him go back
Into the lion. The bitter and the sweet marry.
He himself wronged the lion. Now the wheat
Caresses the wind with its wifely tail; the donkey
Runs in the long grass; and having glimpsed heaven,
The fox's body saunters the tawny earth.

2

After death the soul returns to drinking milk
And honey in its sparse home. Broken lintels
Rejoin the sunrise gates, and bees sing
In the sour meat. Once more in the cradle his
Hair grows long and golden; Delilah's scissors
Turn back into two tiny and playful swords.
Samson, no longer haunted by sunset and shadows,
Sinks down in the eastern ocean and is born.

VISITING MY FATHER

Your chest, hospital gown
Awry, looks
Girlish today.
It is your bluish
Reptile neck
That has known weather.
I said to you, "Are
You ready to die?"
"I am," you said,
"It's too boring
Around here." He has in mind
Some other place
Less boring. "He's
Not ready to go,"
The Doctor said.
There must have been
A fire that nearly
Blew out, or a large
Soul, inadequately
Feathered, that became
Cold and angered.
Some four-year-old boy
In you, chilled by your
Mother, misprized
By your father, said,
"I will defy, I will

Win anyway, I
Will show *them*."
When Alice's well-
Off sister offered to
Take your two boys
During the Depression,
You said it again.
Now you bring that
Defiant mood to death.
The four-year-old
Old man in you does as
He likes: He likes
To stay alive.
Through him you
Get revenge,
Persist, endure,
Overlive, overwhelm,
Get on top.
You gave me
This, and I do
Not refuse it.
It is
In me.

2

My Father at Eighty-Six

You are eighty-
Six, and while we

Talk suddenly
Fall asleep.
Would you have been
Proud of me
If I had lived
More like you?
In this same hospital
Room, drying out
Thirty-five years
Ago, you said to me:
"Are you happy?"
I was twenty-eight.
"Happiness is not one
Of the aims I have
Set for my life."
You were alarmed.
I was bluffing, as
Isolated as you.
Now you have almost
Reached the last station.
Shall I say that you
Misspent your life?
You stood vibrating
On a threshing machine,
Pulleys, choppers, shakers
Beneath you,
And kept your balance
Mostly.
I walked on a rope,

Carrying six
Children on my shoulders,
Felt their love.
A woman had
A message for me
And it arrived.
Now for the first time
I can see your skull
Below your closed
Grape-like eyes.
Some modest,
Luminous
Thing has happened.
Is that all?
What did we expect?

3

The Hard Breathing

Your hard breathing
We all three
Notice. To continue
To live here,
One must take air.
But taking air
Commits you
To sharing it
With the puma and the eagle.
When breathing stops

You will be free
Of that company.
You came from the water
World, and do not
Want to change
Again. My mother
Is not sure where
She wants to be,
But this water world
Is all she can
Remember. Nieces
Are here, nephews,
Classmates, a son.
She sits with puzzled eyes
As if to say,
"Where is that
Reckless man
Who laughed and took
Me from my father?
Is it this man
With gaunt cheeks
On the bed?
All those times
I drove into town,
Carefully, over
Packed snow, is this
What it comes to?" Yes,
Yes, it is, my
Dear Mother.

The tablecloths
You saved are all
Gone; the baked
Corn dish you
Made for your boys,
The Christmas Eves,
Opening perfume—
Evening in Paris—
From your husband,
The hope that a man
Would alter his
Habits for you—
They are all gone.
The nurse takes my father
For his bath.
You and I
Wait here for Jacob
To come back.
"What sort of
Flowers are those?"
"Daisies," I say.
A few minutes later,
You ask again.
What can I do but
Feel time
Go through
Me, and sit
Here with you?

4

Something Has Come

My mother and I sit
In the hospital room.
What can we say
To each other?
That we are nothing
When the Man
Leaves the room?
That we are bound
By our breathing
To this troubled place?
That I am a son
And you are a mother,
And that something
Has come
Between us,
So that we forget
What has saved us.

5

The Komodo Dragon

My father and I
Swim a half mile
Or so apart
In a cold sea.
Each of us senses

The other's strokes,
But we swim far from
The care of women.
I swim on, asking
My shoulders why
My lower half
Feels so heavy.
Only my arms
Lift, the ocean
Pulls the rest
Of me down.
I know that far
Below us, scattered
On the ocean floor,
There are Model A
Engines, spoked wheels
From horse rakes,
Engine blocks
Broken apart,
Snapped plough
Shares, drive shafts
Sticking from sand,
Useless cutter-bars.
Our failures have
Solidified there,
Rusting
In saline water.
We worked all day
Through till mid-

Night and couldn't
Keep the swather
Going, nothing helps,
Drove a piston
Right through the block.
It won't do.
And behind us
A large beast
Swims—four or
Five miles back,
Spines on his nose,
Fins like the
Komodo dragon,
Spiny whiskers,
Following us.

6

The Pharaoh's Servant

My father's large ears
Hear everything.
A hermit wakes
And sleeps in a hut
Underneath
His gaunt cheeks.
His eyes blue, alert,
Disappointed,
And suspicious,
Complain I

I do not bring him
The same sort of
Jokes the nurses
Do. He is a bird
Waiting to be fed—
Mostly beak—an eagle
Or a vulture,
Or the Pharaoh's servant
Just before death.
My arm on the bedrail
Rests there, relaxed,
With new love. All
I know of the Troubadours
I bring to this bed.
I do not want
Or need to be shamed
By him any longer.
The general of shame
Has discharged
Him, and left him
In this small provincial
Egyptian town.
If I do not wish
To shame him, then
Why not love him?
His long hands,
Large, veined,
Capable, can still
Retain hold of what

He wanted:
Six farms. But
Is that what he
Desired? Some
Powerful engine
Of desire goes on
Turning inside his body.
He never phrased
What he desired,
And I am
His son.

7

Prayer for My Father

Your head is still
Restless, rolling
East and west—
That body in you
Insisting on living
Is the old hawk
For whom the world
Darkens. If I
Am not with you
When you die,
That would be grievous
But just. That part
Of you cleaned
My bones more
Than once. But I

Will meet you
In the young hawk
Whom I see
Inside both
You and me.
He has guided
You into the wild—
And will guide
You now to
The Lord of Night,
Who will give
You the tenderness
You wanted here.

In the Funeral Home

1

I missed the hour of your death.
The coffin lid
Lifted shows some
Fall oak leaves sewn
High above
Your winter face.

I have leisure at
Last near
Your cream-colored hands.
I write down what you did,
Or did wrong, or did
Not do at all.

The funeral director, a kind
Man, says, "I'll
Go upstairs now
With my family. You sit as long
As you like.
No one is here."

2

Did I tell you that I regret
Being so agreeable
To you in childhood?
I left at seventeen,
A mother's boy,

Dreamy, smart.
I moved back at twenty-
Eight, with a
Wife, a half
Mile from you. By then
I had found out
What I wanted.

I said it in a poem:
"I want to have
No wife, build
A house with one door,
Be called
Away by wind."

3

You spoke seldom of the Prince
Of Wales, whom
You admired.
He too wanted something
More — and
He had to steal it.

An old man said to me:
"Your father was
The only man
In the county
Who read books
During the Depression."

What good was all that
Seeing we did,
So as to miss
Pheasant nests as we
Mowed or rocks
As we plowed?

I lay my palm on
Your chest. Your chest
Is thin below
The burial suit,
A chicken's breast
Below my hand.

Do we have time for
Each other now?
Do you have
Time for me? Seeing
Is good, as Marvell
Said, but eyes

Are also for weeping.
As I stand next
To you in your long
Coffin, I see we
Have more time
Than we can use.

A WEEK AFTER YOUR DEATH

I dreamt last night you
Lived nearby, not
Dead at all, but safe
In a blacksmith's storage room,
With bolts and nails in bins
From floor to ceiling.

You came and brought me
An ivory jar,
Holding a precious fluid,
Which I took. I knew it meant
The time had come,
But I let you leave.

Later a man pushed open
The door and threw
Your body down, a wizened,
Astonishingly small body—
Rope still tied
Around the neck.

I woke and cried to my wife:
"He didn't die
That way! There was no rope!
All that is wrong!" She
Said, "In
Your dream he did."

St. George and the Dragon

The dragon is losing.
He fights on his back
Fiercely, as when a child
Lifts his four feet
To hold off
The insane parent.
His claws grasp
The wooden lance that has
Pierced his thorny
Breast. . . . But too late. . . .

As children, we knew ours
Was a muddy greatness.
We knew our part
Lay with the dragon.

And this girlish knight?
Oh I know him.
I read the New
Testament as I lay
Naked on my bed
As a boy. The knight
Rises up radiant
With his forehead
Eye that sees past
The criminals' gibbet
To the mindful
Towers of the spirit city.

But I now hate
This solar boy
Whom I have been.

This solar knight
Grows victorious
All over the world.
And the dragon? He
Is the great spirit
The alchemists knew of.
He is Joseph, sent down
To the well. Grendel,
What we have forgotten,
Without whom is nothing.

A sculpture made by Bernt Notke
in 1489 for Stockholm Cathedral

WHEN WILLIAM STAFFORD DIED

Well, water goes down the Montana gullies.
"I'll just go around this rock and think
About it later." That's what you said.
When death came, you said, "I'll go there."

There's no sign you'll come back. Sometimes
My father sat up in the coffin and was alive again.
But I think you were born before my father,
And the feet they made in your time were lighter.

One dusk you were gone. Sometimes a fallen tree
Holds onto a rock, if the current is strong.
I won't say my father did that, but I won't
Say he didn't either. I was watching you both.

If all a man does is to watch from the shore,
Then he doesn't have to worry about the current.
But if affection has put us into the stream,
Then we have to agree to where the water goes.

Gratitude to Old Teachers

When we stride or stroll across the frozen lake,
We place our feet where they have never been.
We walk upon the unwalked. But we are uneasy.
Who is down there but our old teachers?

Water that once could take no human weight—
We were students then—holds up our feet,
And goes on ahead of us for a mile.
Beneath us the teachers, and around us the stillness.

THE DARK EGG

A man bends over the gunwales,
Gazes into the sea
Hour after hour, sees
A lion rising upward.
If he looks to the sky, he sees
A dark egg perfectly
Visible in the Crow's
Stickly nest.

When the Terrible Nurse
Took Vincentine by the
Waist, and threw her
Into the ocean, a whale
Poured her into
His copious throat,
And there she lived
Without husband or children.

What does it matter,
Suffering or not! Bad
Parents, or good
Parents, luck or none—
Let us agree to climb
The trunk of the Crow's tree,
And steal the Black
Egg from his nest!

DRINKING THE WATER

When have we had enough?
When we can turn our head,
Say no to the dog-headed,
Furry-nosed, anus-
Eyed god of duty,
Give payback to God.
Friends, remember no one
Can see his own ears.

Mirabai, night after night
Let herself down castle
Walls on saris to visit
Her low-born teacher.
When she washed his old
Feet and drank the water,
Any idiot would know
She did not care.

Glimpsing the grave ahead
The body leaps up,
Cries, "What if death
Wins, what if it all ends!"
Let it end—let the sand
And the ocean part,
Let it be, let
Heaven and earth go their ways.

THOUGHTS IN THE CABIN

Why do I suddenly feel free of panic?
Here a summer afternoon, wind-
Blown lake, a cabin of strong logs.

I can live and die with no more
Fame; I'd like ground to walk on,
A few books, occasionally a storm.

I know stories I can tell, and I may
Or may not. There is more
To learn: the wind and the screen door.

The granary of images, the Norwegian
Lore, the power of Schmad Razum,
Good or evil, success or failure.

Expect something else from me—
Maybe silence—and don't rule out
Misdirection, misinformation.

X

MORNING POEMS

1993-97

Why We Don't Die

In late September many voices
Tell you you will die.
That leaf says it. That coolness.
All of them are right.

Our many souls—what
Can they do about it?
Nothing. They're already
Part of the invisible.

Our souls have been
Longing to go home
Anyway. "It's late," they say.
"Lock the door, let's go."

The body doesn't agree. It says,
"We buried a little iron
Ball under that tree.
Let's go get it."

EARLY MORNING IN YOUR ROOM

It's morning. The brown scoops of coffee, the
    wasplike
Coffee grinder, the neighbors still asleep.
The gray light as you pour gleaming water—
It seems you've traveled years to get here.

Finally you deserve a house. If not deserve
It, have it; no one can get you out. Misery
Had its way, poverty, no money at least.
Or maybe it was confusion. But that's over.

Now you have a room. Those lighthearted books:
The Anatomy of Melancholy, Kafka's *Letter
To His Father*, are all here. You can dance
With only one leg, and see the snowflake falling

With only one eye. Even the blind man
Can see. That's what they say. If you had
A sad childhood, so what? When Robert Burton
Said he was melancholy, he meant he was home.

CALLING YOUR FATHER

There was a boy who never got enough.
You know what I mean. Something
In him longed to find the big
Mother, and he leaped into the sea.

It took a while, but a whale
Agreed to swallow him.
He knew it was wrong, but once
Past the baleen, it was too late.

It's OK. There's a curved library
Inside, and those high
Ladders. People take requests.
It's like the British Museum.

But one has to build a fire.
Maybe it was the romance
Novels he burned. Smoke curls
Up the gorge. She coughs.

And that's it. The boy swims to shore;
It's a fishing town in Alaska.
He finds a telephone booth,
And calls his father. "Let's talk."

THE SHOCKS WE PUT OUR
PITCHFORKS INTO

The shocks said that winter
Was coming. Each stood there,
Said, "I've given myself away.
Take me. It's over."

And we did. With the shiny tips
Of our forks, their handles so
Healthy and elegant,
We slipped each bundle free,

Gave it to the load.
Each bundle was like
A soul, tucked back
Into the cloud of souls.

That's how it will be
After death—such an abundance
Of souls, all together—
None tired, in the heavy wagon.

CONVERSATION WITH THE SOUL

The soul said, "Give me something to look at."
So I gave her a farm. She said,
"It's too large." So I gave her a field.
The two of us sat down.

Sometimes I would fall in love with a lake
Or a pinecone. But I liked her
Most. She knew it.
"Keep writing," she said.

So I did. Each time the new snow fell,
We would be married again.
The holy dead sat down by our bed.
This went on for years.

"This field is getting too small," she said.
"Don't you know anyone else
To fall in love with?"
What would you have said to Her?

THE YELLOW DOT

In memory of Jane Kenyon

God does what she wants. She has very large
Tractors. She lives at night in the sewing room
Doing stitchery. Then chunks of land at mid-
Sea disappear. The husband knows that his wife
Is still breathing. God has arranged the open
Grave. That grave is not what we want,
But to God it's a tiny hole, and he has
The needle, draws thread through it, and soon
A nice pattern appears. The husband cries,
"Don't let her die!" But God says, "I
Need a yellow dot here, near the mailbox."

The husband is angry. But the turbulent ocean
Is like a chicken scratching for seeds. It doesn't
Mean anything, and the chicken's claws will tear
A Rembrandt drawing if you put it down.

Three-Day Fall Rain

The three-day
October rain blows
Leaves down. We knew
That life wouldn't last long.

The dock gleams
With oak leaves, cold
Leaves in the boat, leaves
Spotted in the old man grass.

Hardy warned
Us. Jesus in his boat,
Standing, his back turned,
Being rowed to the other shore.

WHAT JESUS SAID

The wind blows where it likes: that is what
Everyone is like who is born from the wind.
Oh now it's getting serious. We are the ones
Born from the wind that blows along the plains
And over the sea where no one has a home.
And that Upsetting Rabbi, didn't he say:
"Take nothing with you, no blanket, no bread.
When evening comes, sleep wherever you are.
And if the owners say no, shake out the dust
From your sandals; leave the dust on their doorstep."
Don't hope for what will never come. Give up hope,
Dear friends, the joists of life are laid on the winds.

WHEN THRESHING TIME ENDS

There is a time. Things end.
All the fields are clean.
Belts are put away.
And the horses go home.

What is left endures
In the minds of boys
Who wanted this joy
Never to end.

The splashing of hands,
Jokes and oats:
It was a music
Touching and fervent.

The Bible was right.
Presences come and go.
Wash in cold water.
The fire has moved.

TASTING HEAVEN

Some people say that every poem should have
God in it somewhere. But of course Wallace Stevens
Wasn't one of those. We live, he said, "in a world
Without heaven to follow." Shall we agree

That we taste heaven only once, when we see
Her at fifteen walking among falling leaves?
It's possible. And yet as Stevens lay dying
He invited the priest in. There, I've said it.

The priest is not an argument, only an instance.
But our gusty emotions say to me that we have
Tasted heaven many times: these delicacies
Are left over from some larger party.

Wallace Stevens and Florence

Oh Wallace Stevens, dear friend,
You are such a pest. You are so sure.
You think everyone is in *your* family.

It is you and your father and Mozart,
And ladies tasting cold rain in Florence,
Puzzling out inscriptions, studying the gold flake.

It is as if life were a visit to Florence,
A place where there are no maggots in the flesh,
No one screaming, no one afraid.

Your job, your joy, your morning walk—
As if you walked on the wire of the mind,
High above the elephants; you cry out but you never
    fall.

As if we could walk always high above the world,
No bears, no witches, no Macbeth,
No one screaming, no one in pain, no one afraid.

THE WALTZ

One man I know keeps saying that we don't need
Heaven. He thinks embroidered Russian
Wedding blouses will take the place of angels,
Or windy nights when the crows fly up in front
Of your car will replace all the Psalmists.

He wants us to dance high-hearted, like the bacchae,
Even if it's a waltz. It's a little awkward;
But if you practice, he says, you can do it.
The hard thing is to try to figure out how
To say good-bye—even just going to the grocery.

Looking at the Stars

I still think about the shepherds, how many stars
They saw. We owe our love of God to these sheep
That had to be followed, or companioned, all night.
One can't just let them run. By midnight

The stars had already become huge talkers.
The Parent sits in her proud Chair, and is punished.
The Dog follows the Hunter. Each time a story ends
There is such a long pause before another begins.

Those of us who are parents, and getting older,
Long, as tonight, for our children to stand
With us, looking at the stars. Here it is,
Eight thousand years later, and I still remember.

WAKING ON THE FARM

I can remember the early mornings—how the stubble,
A little proud with frost, snapped as we walked.

How the John Deere tractor hood pulled heat
Away from our hands when we filled it with gas.

And the way the sun brought light right out of the
    ground.
It turned on a whole hill of stubble as easily as a single
    stone.

Breathing seemed frail and daring in the morning.
To pull in air was like reading a whole novel.

The angleworms, turned up by the plow, looked
Uneasy like shy people trying to avoid praise.

For a while we had goats. They were like turkeys
Only more reckless. One butted a red Chevrolet.

When we washed up at noon, we were more ordinary.
But the water kept something in it of the early
    morning.

WHAT THE ANIMALS PAID

The Hampshire ewes standing in their wooden pens,
Their shiny black hooves close to each other,

Had to pay with their wool, with their wombs,
With their eating, with their fear of the dogs.

Every animal had to pay. Horses paid all day;
They pulled stone boats and the ground pulled back.

And the pigs? They paid with their squealing
When the knife entered the throat and the blood

Followed it out. The blood, steaming and personal,
Paid it. Any debt left over the intestines paid.

"I am what I am." The pig could not say that.
The women paid with their bowed heads, and the
    men,

My father among them, paid with their drinking.
Demons shouted: "Pay to the last drop!" I paid

The debt another way. Because I did not pay
In the farm way, I am writing this poem today.

FOR RUTH

There's a graceful way of doing things. Birch branches
Curve slightly upward; or the wind brings a few
Snowflakes down, and then joins the night;
Or you leave me a sprig of chervil and no more.

Each morning we have this new chance. We can walk
A few steps behind the others down the mountain;
We can enter a conversation as if we were blessed,
Not insisting on our old way of gaining pity.

There's a way you have of knowing what another
May need ahead of time, before the party
Begins, as smoke sometimes disappears
Downward among branches. And I've learned

From you this new way of letting a poem be.

THE MAN WHO DIDN'T KNOW
WHAT WAS HIS

There was a man who didn't know what was his.
He thought as a boy that some demon forced him
To wear "his" clothes and live in "his" room
And sit on "his" chair and be a child of "his" parents.

Each time he sat down to dinner, it happened again.
His own birthday party belonged to someone else.
And—was it sweet potatoes that he liked?—
He should resist them. Whose plate is this?

This man will be like a lean-to attached
To a house. It doesn't *have* a foundation.
This man is helpful and hostile in each moment.
This man leans toward you and leans away.

Maybe you've met this man who doesn't know what
    is his.

Thinking About Old Jobs

Well, let's say this morning is all of life there is—
Let's suppose the weather (rainy), the room
(Creamy-walled), the bed (soft), your cells (calm,
Excitable and dense) are it. Don't expect more.

Then what? Does it matter how you chose
To live at twenty? You felt detached, let's say,
So you blew your legs and arms off.
Why feel bad? It helped in some ways.

You had more solitude, because friends avoid stumps.
Of course you had to live. You started picking
Other people's cucumbers with your teeth,
As you lay flat on a board. Don't be ashamed.

It was a deal. It worked. The boss's children
Later sent you back the canceled contract.
Then remember the job you had lying about
Your health to life insurance companies?

Or performing as a Santa in Depression wards?
All those jobs were all right. But that time is over.
Am I content? I am. But we don't
Have to live in the way we did then: Let's talk.

CONVERSATION WITH A MONSTER

A man I knew could never say who he was.
You know people like that. When he met a monster,
He'd encourage the monster to talk about eating
But failed to say that he objected to being prey.

A day goes by; a week; a month; it's summer.
The adolescent wolverines go out scouting;
Crabs lift their claws; the praying mantis
Get religious. This man keeps trying to adapt.

Adopt? Be adopted? It's funny, but those born
From eggs seem not to feel homeless. Something
Pushes them out, and they fly to sea, or swim
Up from the gravel, milkily transparent, and they're
    gone.

This man went up to monsters and asked to be
Adopted. I've done that often. Reader, are you
Fond of the Jonah story? Say to a monster,
"I may have something for you, but I can't promise."

The Resemblance Between Your Life and a Dog

I never intended to have this life, believe me—
It just happened. You know how dogs turn up
At a farm, and they wag but can't explain.

It's good if you can accept your life—you'll notice
Your face has become deranged trying to adjust
To it. Your face thought your life would look

Like your bedroom mirror when you were ten.
That was a clear river touched by mountain wind.
Even your parents can't believe how much you've
    changed.

Sparrows in winter, if you've ever held one, all
    feathers,
Burst out of your hand with a fiery glee.
You see them later in hedges. Teachers praise you,

But you can't quite get back to the winter sparrow.
Your life is a dog. He's been hungry for miles,
Doesn't particularly like you, but gives up, and
    comes in.

It Is So Easy to Give In

I have been thinking about the man who gives in.
Have you heard about him? In his story
A twenty-eight-foot pine meets a small wind
And the pine bends all the way over to the ground.

"I was persuaded," the pine says. "It was convincing."
A mouse visits a cat, and the cat agrees
To drown all her children. "What could I do?"
The cat said. "The mouse *needed* that."

It's strange. I've heard that some people conspire
In their own ruin. A fool says, "You don't
Deserve to live." The man says, "I'll string this rope
Over that branch, maybe you can find a box."

The Great One with her necklace of skulls says,
"I need twenty thousand corpses." "Tell you what,"
The General says, "we have an extra battalion
Over there on the hill. We don't need all these men."

The Green Cookstove

A lonely man once sat on a large flat stone.
When he lifted it, he saw a kitchen: a green
Enamel range with big claw feet, familiar.
Someone lives in that room, cooking and cackling.

"I saw her once," Virgil said. "She and Helen
Were sisters." Helen's husband, Menelaus,
Sits by the window, peeling garlic cloves,
And throwing bread crusts to the chickens.

We'll never understand this. Somewhere below
The flat stone of the skull, a carnivorous couple
Lives and plans future wars. Are we innocent?
These wars don't happen by accident—they occur

Too regularly. How often do we lift the plate
At the bottom of our brain and throw some garlic
And grain down to the kitchen? "Keep cooking,
My dears," we say. "Something good will come of this."

THE RUSSIAN

"The Russians had few doctors on the front line.
My father's job was this: After the battle
Was over, he'd walk among the men hit,
Sit down and ask: 'Would you like to die on your
Own in a few hours, or should I finish it?'
Most said, 'Don't leave me.' The two would have
A cigarette. He'd take out his small notebook—
We had no dog tags, you know—and write the man's
Name down, his wife's, his children, his address, and
        what
He wanted to say. When the cigarette was done,
The soldier would turn his head to the side. My father
Finished off four hundred men that way during the
        war.
He never went crazy. They were his people.

"He came to Toronto. My father in the summers
Would stand on the lawn with a hose, watering
The grass that way. It took a long time. He'd talk
To the moon, to the wind. 'I can hear you growing'—
He'd say to the grass. 'We come and go.
We're no different from each other. We are all
Part of something. We have a home.' When I was
        thirteen,
I said, 'Dad, do you know they've invented sprinklers
Now?' He went on watering the grass.
'This is my life. Just shut up if you don't understand
        it.'"

THE FACE IN THE TOYOTA

Suppose you see a face in a Toyota
One day, and you fall in love with that face,
And it is Her, and the world rushes by
Like dust blown down a Montana street.

And you fall upward into some deep hole,
And you can't tell God from a grain of sand.
And your life is changed, except that now you
Overlook even more than you did before;

And these ignored things come to bury you,
And you are crushed, and your parents
Can't help anymore, and the woman in the Toyota
Becomes a part of the world that you don't see.

And now the grain of sand becomes sand again,
And you stand on some mountain road weeping.

TWO WAYS TO WRITE POEMS

"I am who I am." I wonder what one has to pay
To say that. I couldn't do it. For years
I thought, "You are who you are." But maybe
You weren't. Maybe you were someone else.

Sam's friend, who loved poetry, played football
In school even though he didn't want to.
He got hit. Later he said to me, "I write poems.
I am who I am . . . but my neck hurts."

How many times I have begun a poem
Before I knew what the main sounds
Would be. We find out. Toward the end
The poem is just beginning to be who it is.

That's all right, but there's another way as well.
One picks the rhyme words, and so the main
Sounds, before one begins. I wonder what
Yeats had to pay in order to do that.

ONE SOURCE OF BAD INFORMATION

There's a boy in you about three
Years old who hasn't learned a thing for thirty
Thousand years. Sometimes it's a girl.

This child had to make up its mind
How to save you from death. He said things like:
"Stay home. Avoid elevators. Eat only elk."

You live with this child, but you don't know it.
You're in the office, yes, but live with this boy
At night. He's uninformed, but he does want

To save your life. And he has. Because of this boy
You survived a lot. He's got six big ideas.
Five don't work. Right now he's repeating them to
    you.

My Doubts on Going to Visit
a New Friend

I'm glad that a white horse grazes in that meadow
Outside your kitchen window; even when it rains
There's still someone there. And it rains often
In the mountains.

I have to ask myself what kind of friend I can be.
You'll want to know whether I do dishes,
Or know my share of stories, or any Wallace
Stevens poems by heart.

I know that I won't talk all the time, or steal
Money, or complain about my room,
Or undermine you, or speak disparagingly
Of your family.

I am afraid there'll be a moment when
I fail you, friend; I will turn slightly
Away, our eyes will not meet, and out in the field
There will be no one.

For John

VISITING SAND ISLAND

Somebody showed off and tried to tell the truth
And drank wine and went to bed. Someone
Woke in the night and wanted his children
To walk in the grass on this island under the stars.

Someone was lucky. Someone had eyes and found
Stars. Someone had feet and found grass.
Someone loved thought, and knew things to learn.
Somone could turn in the river and go up or down.

Someone thought he was unlucky, thought he didn't
    try
To tell the truth. Someone thought his head was dark.
Someone tried to feel as bad as others did; someone
Flapped along the ground to draw the fox to him.

Tell him, friends, that the nest is now gone;
Tell him the little twigs are all dispersed.
Tell him all he has to do is walk under stars.
Tell him the fox has long since eaten his dinner.

A WEEK OF POEMS AT BENNINGTON

SUNDAY

The Dog's Ears

A little snow. Coffee. The bowled-over branches,
The wind; it is cold outdoors; but in the bed
It's warm, in the early lamplight, reading poems.

These fingers, so rosy, so alive, move about
This book. Here is my wide-traveling palm,
The thumb that looks like my father's, the wedding ring.

It's time to prepare myself, as a friend suggested,
"Not to be here." It will happen. People will say,
"That day the dish lay empty on the brown table.

"The gold knob shone alone in the dark.
The light came in, and no eyes received it,
And bits of ice hung on the dog's ears."

MONDAY

When the Cat Stole the Milk

Well there it is. There's nothing to do.
The cat steals the milk and it's gone.
Then the cat steals you, and you're found
Days later, with milk on your face.

That implies that you become whoever
Steals you. The trees steal a man,
And an old birch becomes his wife
And they live together in the woods.

Some of us have always wanted
God to steal us. Then our friends
Would call each other, and print
Posters, and we would never be found.

TUESDAY

Being Happy All Night

It's as if the mice stayed warm inside the snow,
As if my cells heard laughing from the Roman
    vineyards.
Mice slept despite the cruel songs of the stars.
We laughed and woke and sniffed and slept again.

Some people inside my body last night
Married each other just in order to dance.
And Sara Grethe smiled so proudly the men
Kicked their heels on the planks, but kept the beat.

Oh I think it was the books I read long ago.
It's as if I joined other readers on a long road.
We found dead men hanging in a meadow.
We took dew from the grass and washed our eyes.

For S. B.

WEDNESDAY

The Widowed Friend

For D. H.

I hear rustlings from the next room; and he is ready
To leave. "See you tomorrow." A long line
Of feeling follows him out the door. He carries
On his shoulders—which slope a little—a divorce,

Prosody, marital love as pertinacious
As a bulldog's mouth, a grandfather, grand-
Mother. Land and death weigh him down, so he
Becomes a large man on a thin bridge walking.

If, now, he lives alone, who will hear
The thin cough in the morning, who will hear
The milk hitting the pail when the old man sings?
Who will notice the forty drafts on yellow paper?

It's up to us to see him, call him, and say,
"Stay, friend, be with us, tell me what happened."

THURSDAY

We Only Say That

"There are so many things to love around here."
We only say that when we want to hint
Something—the day after we notice a woman,
Who waves a hand with her female bravery.

We say, "The icicles are really brilliant today!"
Or, "Let's make fun of other people."
That would bring us closer. Or "Martha brought
Her dog out into the morning snow."

Her hand reaches up to brush her neck,
Or she puts on her boots. A voice inside us
Says, "Oh a woman! Let's close the door.
Let's flirt and not flirt. Let's play cards and laugh."

FRIDAY

Wounding Others

Well I do it, and it's done.
And it can't be taken back.
There's a wound in my chest
Where I wounded others.

But it will knit, or heal, in time.
That's what you say.
And some that I wounded
Claim: "I am the better for it."

Was it truth-telling or
A messiah with a knife?
The wound will close, or heal
In time. That's what you say.

SATURDAY

What the Buttocks Think

Don't tell me that nothing can be done.
The tongue says, "I know I can change things."
The toe says, "I have my ways."
The heart is weeping and remembering Eden.

Legs think that a good run will do it.
Tongue has free tickets; he'll fly to heaven.
But the buttocks see everything upside down:
They want you to put your head down there,

Remind the heart it was upside down
In the womb, so that when your mother,
Knowing exactly where she was going,
Walked upstairs, you weren't going anywhere.

ALL THESE STORIES

There are so many stories. In one, a bear
Marries a sailing ship, and they have children
Who are islands (covered with low brush).
In another an obstinate woman floats upstream.

Or the child wailing on a rock, set ashore
By her seal mother (her real mother), waits
And wails, and faces appear at windows until
Charlotte Brontë agrees to begin her novel.

You know stories like that. The Terrible Nurse
Throws the Daughter into the sea. A whale
Swallows her, and she is free from husband
And children long enough to be herself.

Something in us wants things to happen.
We bend our ankle and end up reading Gibbon.
In some dreams a wolf pursues us until we
Turn into swallows, and agree to live in longing.

THINGS TO THINK

Think in ways you've never thought before.
If the phone rings, think of it as carrying a message
Larger than anything you've ever heard,
Vaster than a hundred lines of Yeats.

Think that someone may bring a bear to your door,
Maybe wounded and deranged; or think that a moose
Has risen out of the lake, and he's carrying on his
    antlers
A child of your own whom you've never seen.

When someone knocks on the door, think that he's
    about
To give you something large: tell you you're forgiven,
Or that it's not necessary to work all the time, or that
    it's
Been decided that if you lie down no one will die.

THE GLIMPSE OF SOMETHING
IN THE OVEN

Childhood is like a kitchen. It is dangerous
To the mice, but the husband gets fed; he's
An old giant, grumbling and smelling children.
The kitchen is a place where you get smaller

And smaller, or you lose track. In general
You become preoccupied with this old lady
In the kitchen. . . . She putters about, opens oven
   doors.
The thing is the old woman won't *discuss* anything.

The giant will. He's always been a fan of Aristotle,
Knew him at school. It is no surprise to him
That the Trojan War lasted ten years, or how it
Ended. He knows something you don't.

Your sister says, "Say, what's that in the oven?"

It's As If Someone Else Is with Me

1

It's as if someone else is here with me, here in this
    room
In which I lie. The longing the ear feels for sound
Has given me the sweetness that I confuse with Her.

The joy of being alone, eating the honey of words.
The white-walled room, and Stevens, and the sun.
This is the joy of the soul that has preserved
Itself despite fleas and soap in the lighthearted sun.

One is not alone when one is alone, if She
Is here. It is a She that no one loves, a She
That one loves when one loves what one does love.

5

I've been thinking about these little adventures
In morning longing—these embarkations,
Excursions in round hide boats on the sea,
Passing over the beings far below.

The deep vowels—perhaps whales—mourn
And sing at their stone table five miles down
On the ocean floor. They mourn some loss.
But the small finny sounds, the *ers* and *ins*

And *ors* and *ings,* mourn as well—we don't
Know what. Perhaps vowels were all created
In a moment of sorrow before creation—
A grief they've not been able to sing in this life.

7

It's good to remain in bed awhile, and listen
For the *ay* slyly hidden in sequacious,
And scent in summer world the two *ers.*
I especially love the *in* hidden in wood bins.

Am I like the hog snuffling for truffles,
Followed by skimpy lords in oversized furs?
For this gaiety do I need forgiveness?
Does the lark need forgiveness for its blue eggs?

So it's a birdlike thing then, this warming
And hiding of sounds. They are the little low
Heavens in the nest; now my chest feathers
Widen, now I'm an old hen, now I am satisfied.

248

WHEN MY DEAD FATHER CALLED

Last night I dreamt my father called to us.
He was stuck somewhere. It took us
A long time to dress, I don't know why.
The night was snowy; there were long black roads.

Finally, we reached the little town, Bellingham.
There he stood, by a streetlamp in cold wind,
Snow blowing along the sidewalk. I noticed
The uneven sort of shoes that men wore

In the early Forties. And overalls. He was smoking.
Why did it take us so long to get going? Perhaps
He left us somewhere once, or did I simply
Forget he was alone in winter in some town?

WORDS THE DREAMER SPOKE TO MY
FATHER IN MAINE

Ocean light as we wake reminds us how dark
Our old house is. That's home. Like Hamlet,
One visit to Wittenberg is enough, and we'll soon be
Back in crazy Denmark. I dreamt I stood

In a machine shop; my dead father stands beside me.
We talk, but his eyes remain on my chest.
I say to him for the first time: "Oh look at me
When we talk." I could see cubbyholes

With dark tools, and a rough floor stained with oil.
Clotted windows, cobwebs, a black vise.
But sunlight outside our windows speaks of ocean
Light, bone light, Labrador light, prairie light.

It's the same light that glints off swords, and shines
From Idaho rivers some days, and from the thin
Face just before death. I say to my father,
"We could be there if we could lift our eyes."

LOOKING AT AGING FACES

Some faces get older and remain who they are. Oh
You can see disappointment there, where parent-
    teacher
Meetings have affected the chin; or the nose got
    pushed
To one side by deaths. So many things happen:
People move away, or your mother becomes crazy
And bites the nurse.

Each face had a long time in the womb to decide
How much it would let worldly things affect it,
How often it would turn toward the wall or the
    woods,
So it didn't have to be seen, how much
It would give in, how stubbornly it would
Hold its own.

Some faces remain whole and radiant. We study them
To find a clue. Aunt Nettie said, "My father
Put on cuff links every day." Memories like that
Help. One face, as firmly profiled as a hawk,
Used to say: "The world is fair, and if it's not,
I think it is."

For some of us, insults sink in, or the feet
Inherit two roads and lose the way; for others, cold
And hunger come. Some faces change. It's not wrong.
And if you look carefully, you can see,
By glimpsing us just after we wake,
Who we are.

For Bill and Nancy

A Christmas Poem

Christmas is a place, like Jackson Hole. We all agree
To meet there once a year. It has water, and grass for
    horses;
All the fur traders can come in. We visited the place
As children, but we never heard the good stories.

Those stories only get told in the big tents, late
At night, when a trapper who has been caught
In his own trap, held down in icy water, talks, and a
    man
With a ponytail and a limp comes in from the edge of
    the fire.

As children, we knew there was more to it—
Why some men got drunk on Christmas Eve
Wasn't explained, nor why we were so often
Near tears or why the stars came down so close,

Why so much was lost. Those men and women
Who had died in wars for a thousand years,
Did they come that night? Is that why the Christmas
    tree
Trembled just before we opened the presents?

There was something about angels. *Angels we have*
Heard on high Sweetly singing o'er the plains.
The angels were certain. But we were not
Certain if our family tonight was worthy.

PEOPLE LIKE US

For James Wright

There are more like us. All over the world
There are confused people, who can't remember
The name of their dog when they wake up, and
    people
Who love God but can't remember where

He was when they went to sleep. It's
All right. The world cleanses itself this way.
A wrong number occurs to you in the middle
Of the night, you dial it, it rings just in time

To save the house. And the second-story man
Gets the wrong address, where the insomniac lives,
And he's lonely, and they talk, and the thief
Goes back to college. Even in graduate school,

You can wander into the wrong classroom,
And hear great poems lovingly spoken
By the wrong professor. And you find your soul,
And greatness has a defender, and even in death
    you're safe.

THE NEURONS WHO WATCH BIRDS

We have to think now what it would be like
To be old. Some funny little neurons,
Developed for high-speed runners, and quick-
Handed bowmen, begin to get tired. They fire

But then lay down their bows and watch birds.
The kidney cells—"Too much thinking!" the Chinese
Say—look around for help, but the kids have
All gone to the city. Your friends get hit by lightning,

And your enemies live on. This isn't going to get
Better. Crows yelling from the telephone wires
Don't include you in the stories they tell, and they
        seem
To remember some story that you haven't heard.

What can you do? We'll have to round up
All those little people wandering about
In the body, get them to sit up straight, and study
This problem: How *do* we die?

BAD PEOPLE

A man told me once that all the bad people
Were needed. Maybe not all, but your fingernails
You need; they are really claws, and we know
Claws. The sharks—what about them?
They make other fish swim faster. The hard-faced men
In black coats who chase you for hours
In dreams—that's the only way to get you
To the shore. Sometimes those hard women
Who abandon you get you to say, "You."
A lazy part of us is like a tumbleweed.
It doesn't move on its own. Sometimes it takes
A lot of Depression to get tumbleweeds moving.
Then they blow across three or four States.
This man told me that things work together.
Bad handwriting sometimes leads to new ideas;
And a careless god—who refuses to let people
Eat from the Tree of Knowledge—can lead
To books, and eventually to us. We write
Poems with lies in them, but they help a little.

Wanting More Applause at a Conference

It's something about envy. I won't say I'm envious,
But I did have certain moods when I was two.
Now of course I can't remember any of that.
I'm happy if another receives some praise or attention

That's really mine. I talk, and the man next to me
Talks, and he gets the applause. Or I am confused
And she makes sense. This is hard to bear.
I bear it, but it causes trouble inside the den.

Is it a mammal problem then? Six teats are palpable
Far inside the wiry fur, and I want more
Than one? Is that it? It is, but such greed
Is mainly a problem for small mammals.

And I am no longer small. Let's call it a mood
When we can't remember. Let's call it a habit
Of opening the mouth when we, who have
Much, want more, even what belongs to the poor.

A Conversation with a Mouse

One day a mouse called to me from his curly nest:
"How do you sleep? I love curliness."

"Well, I like to be stretched out—I like the bones to be
All lined up. I like to see my toes way off over there."

"I suppose that's one way," he said, "but I don't like it.
The planets don't act that way—nor the Milky Way."

What could I say? You know you're near the end
Of the century when a sleepy mouse brings in the
   Milky Way.

XI

NEW POEMS

1997–98

POEM FOR EUDALIA

When I was twenty-five it was Eudalia
Who saved me. She was the Queen
Of fire and snow. She was the dark
Christian in the ghazals of love.

She mingled the perfume of her breasts
With the alphabet; and forgave young boys.
She was the Cleopatra in the church aisle,
A sprig of chervil on the Archbishop's bed.

I heard Eudalia say, "Let Jesus leave
His mother and come to me!"
The Judas vines grow from the belly.
The world is light in every dark hair.

GOING HOME WITH THE WORLD

Well, the world catches us.
One birdcall and we're in
It again. We say to
The world: "Let's go

To your place." The world
Says, "Okay." A necklace
Of ocean shells hangs
On the bedroom wall,

A sea urchin with a light inside
On a shelf, and the paws of a tiger.
Well, let's get comfortable!
But soon that absent tiger

Will come—the one who's
Been missing her paws. . . .

An Afternoon in June

The father sits on a chair and looks down at the
    ground.
It will come, my dears. The femur leads
To the kneecap, and New Zealand is not
Far behind. Today is her day in June.

It's spring and I'm free. Curtains stretch
Out before the window like girls on a picnic.
No one's grandmother has died. The boys
Still hold in them the seeds of Roncevaux.

New people have taken over the motel. It's
All right. What right did we have to throw
Tires into the river? Plotinus nursed
Until he was eleven. He saw the Mother

And she is the hardest to see. The hawk's mother's
Wing feathers shine. My mother's soul is gone.
Some invisible sweetness holds the knee
And the kneecap together, and despite Plotinus

Or because of him, the fire in the heart
Continues burning. Her soul lives in the sparkles
Of sunshine in the curtains now and in the wind.
The father sits in a chair and looks down.

A POEM BEGINNING WITH A LINE BY
SEAL SCHOLARS

"Elephant seals have a serious Oedipal problem."
All that young male flesh, snorting and whiskered,
Sprawls on lank rocks, waiting years for the big
Bulls to die. It's ignoble. Over on the next shelf,
They can see plump women with their faces turned
Away, like those whose angels who would not sing to
    Milton.

Oh, Milton! He was a dear elephant seal always
Longing for Virgil's rock. He's snorting there now,
Rearranging himself and hoping that his insults
To the pagan gods will be overlooked.
And Emily Dickinson, how does she feel about this—
Looking across and seeing Milton with his long face?

For Nils Peterson

THE DOG THAT PURSUES US

Oh well. The man whose head thinks on a pillow,
Filled with goosy down, all night
Knows, or tries to know, if we are
What we say we are. The down says no.

We turn this way and that, trying to escape
Our childhood, which keeps pursuing us.
It's like a dog! And we are the master,
Running on ahead in the high mountain air.

Oh dog, come closer. We've climbed up so
High we've passed the sheep pens; and now
We're dislodging stones. And still the dog
Keeps nosing our feet up the mountain.

We could climb higher but that would only
Make more work for the dog. Haven't we
Given enough of ourselves to the high air?
The ancients would long ago have gone down.

THE DAY WE VISITED NEW ORLEANS

So much time has gone by! Napoleon's house—
He never came—still stands in the Quarter.
Time ends all the good living that
Louis the Sixteenth, after the trouble, never
Experienced, all the sights Andrew
Jackson never saw in Pirate's Alley.
Ask the alligators about heat and history.

Out in the bayous we met a small alligator
Named Elvis. When we stroked his throat, he waved
His left claw at the world. It makes you think.
Alligators enjoy a world before the alphabet.

I don't want to be who you are! I want
To be myself, someone playing with language.
Let us each be a sensualist
Of the imponderable! Let's each do
What we want. I thread my way
Down alphabets to the place where Elvis is.

A Dog, a Policeman, and the Spanish Poetry Reading

Plaza de Santa Ana, Las Palmas

Tonight I heard a small noisy dog barking
As the Macedonian poet gave—in Macedonian—his
    poem.
A policeman dressed in his cloudlike uniform
Walked slowly toward the dog, saying with his body:
"Leave us now. Go down this little alley.
Important things are happening here—old ladies
Are listening . . . things you wouldn't understand."

Above us on the high building front four white
    women
Entrusted with Justice and Injustice, War and Art,
Hold up their shields as if to say, "On earth
Men only want us to keep them from barking.
Up here we are alone but separate from the dogs."

After a short silence, the loose little dog began
To bark again, ignoring the rhythm of the poets.
By now a Castillian poet was speaking—
Probably concealing his bark, as we all do—
Those great words *la muerte, la mar, eternidad.*
His wavelike singing out of *la eternidad* suggested
—In some way that none of us could understand—
That we as human beings are better than we are.
The assuring sounds of the great words

Carried us as in a small pony cart away
From the orphanage. It took us farther from truth.
Suddenly I admired Antonio Machado even more
Who in his poems had broken this sleep of vowels.
I could see Antonio in his black coat slowly climb out
Of the pony cart, and walk back toward the
    orphanage.

For Louis

Thinking of *Gitanjali*

A man is walking along thinking of *Gitanjali*,
And a mink leaps out from under a log. I don't know
Why it is I want you to sit on my lap,
Or why it is our children speak to us lovingly.

Answering that is like plotting one's
Political life by listening to Schubert, or letting
The length of your poem be decided by how
Many times the goldfish turns in his bowl.

I do remember that boy in the third grade
Who said, "We're friends, but let's fight!"
So affection intricately inserts itself.
The story makes sense, I guess, like everything

Else that happened when you were
On your way to school. And those gestures
Of love our mother gave us we saved
Somewhere, as Tagore did, until they

Became evidence of the love of God.

The Donkey's Ear

I've been talking into the ear of a donkey.
I have so much to say, and the donkey can't wait
To feel my breath stirring the immense oats
Of his ears. "What has happened to the spring,"
I say, "and our legs that were so joyful
In the bobblings of April?" I do feel teenier
As if some taut giant, once at the center
Of things, had moved to Sweden. Am I an ant
Struggling to lift a dark barn
Off its base? Am I changing my road
So that I can play with the old moonlight
Once more, and be what I once was, a lover
Whispering, struggling to catch fur in my hands
So I can lift my lips closer to the donkey's ear?